ACE YOUR TEACHER RESUME
(and Cover Letter)

Anthony D. Fredericks, Ed.D.
www.anthonydfredericks.com

BLUE RIVER PRESS

Indianapolis, Indiana

Ace Your Teacher Resume (and Cover Letter)

Published by Blue River Press
Indianapolis, Indiana
www.brpressbooks.com

Distributed by Cardinal Publishers Group
317-352-8200 phone
317-352-8202 fax
www.cardinalpub.com

ISBN: 978-1-68157-020-4

Author: Anthony D. Fredericks, Ed.D.
Editor: Dani McCormick
Book Design: Dave Reed
Cover Design: Phil Velikan
Cover Photos: shutterstock_86718250; shutterstock_272513510
Publication Date: 2017

Printed in the United States of America

Dedication

Here's to my fellow Senior Spartans
(AKA "The Breakfast Boys")
for their steadfast support
and constant camaraderie:
Bob Lindsay, Pete Piepmeier, & Mike McGough.

Contents

Acknowledgements

The term "strength in numbers" is a viable component for any social enterprise; so too, does it hold true in the writing of a book. No book can truly be the sole enterprise of the author whose name appears on the cover. Each publication is a reflection of many minds, many thoughts, and many insights. I have been quite fortunate in this literary journey to have been able to tap into the collective wisdom of many individuals who have added immeasurably to this endeavor. I am eternally grateful for their perceptions, thoughts, and recommendations…and equally richer for their professionalism and camaraderie.

My colleagues in the Department of Education at York College of Pennsylvania have, over the years, endured all manner of questions, ruminations, and discussions. They have "suffered gladly" with my intellectual inquiries, off-the-wall probes, and investigative conversations. They are to be celebrated for their endurance as well as for their camaraderie. Here's to Stacey Dammann, Katie Beauchat, Josh DeSantis, Nicole Hesson, Leah Kocoronis, Kim Sutton, Becky Speelman, Amy Glusco, Leslie Trimmer, and Sherry Rankin. What an incredible team!

So too, do all my undergraduate students at York College deserve a standing round of applause! They have "endured" my persistent (higher-level) questioning, intense discussions, and verbal inquisitions for several decades now – all with good cheer and professional dedication. That they will influence a new generation of scholars is a given; that they will also make a difference in the education profession is equally assured. It is my constant honor and privilege to work with them in pursuit of their dreams.

To all the school administrators (active and retired) I encountered on this journey, I offer a most grateful "high five" along with my eternal gratitude. Your opinions and preferences about what goes into quality resumes and equally dynamic cover letters is truly appreciated as much as it is celebrated. Many thanks go out to Pete Piepmeier, Mike McGough, Bob Lindsay, Scott Krauser, Sue Cathcart, Jamie Kerstetter, Susan Seiple, Charles Patterson, Sarah Vaux, Kim Stoltz, Scott Carl,

Lawrence Sanders, Kevin Peters, Allan Decort, Ken Armacost, Jon Weaver, Melanie Simmons, Russ Greenholt, Wes Doll, Alicia Warren, Stephanie Ferree, Karen Kugler, Ken Stanhauser, Mark Maldet, Robert Shick, and Bruce Sanborn.

For the resume blunders, confusions, and just plain silliness included in the "A Touch of Humor" entries a tip of the hat and a note of appreciation goes out to the following entities: Jobmob; Careerbuilder; Resume Bloopers; Ask Annie; Resumepower; Hotjob; Humormatters; Resumaina's Archive; and Askreddit. Thanks for all the fun, guys.

And to you, the reader, I extend my personal thanks for adding this book to your personal library. It is my sincere hope that the advice and suggestions in these pages will help you realize your career goals and ensure your dream of becoming a classroom teacher. May all your professional wishes come true and may you reap all the benefits of these words. I look forward to your entry into this grand and glorious profession of ours. Welcome aboard!

Introduction

Let's begin this book with a bold statement from a professional recruiter who has personally reviewed more than 20,000 teacher resumes and cover letters over the past 13 years:

> *The overwhelming majority of resumes and cover letters are mediocre and often passed over. Many candidates may have been really interesting people who could change students' lives, but the resumes were cluttered, disorganized, and didn't tell a story specific and unique to them.*[1]

One look at the statement above and you may be inclined to throw up your hands and say something like: "OMG, there's no hope for me!" However, I'd like to invite you to look at that statement in a positive vein. That is, keep in mind that most of your competition for a potential teaching position will submit <u>mediocre</u> resumes and <u>mediocre</u> cover letters. They will be the ones who submit resumes that are "cluttered, disorganized, and [don't] tell a story specific and unique to [the applicant]." You, on the other hand, will be able to positively distinguish yourself from the completion; because, with this book

You will *ace your teacher resume (and cover letter)!*

As you'll learn in Chapter 1, the resume is perhaps the most important document you can craft in your pursuit of the ideal teaching position. Send in a resume that clearly places you at the head of the pack, front of the line, top of the heap, ahead of the curve (please select your own idiom) and you will have initiated a process that will have school administrators clamoring to get you in for an interview (which you will also be able to <u>ace</u> with the *Ace Your Teacher Interview* [same author] book) and bring you on board as a full-time teacher. Submit a resume similar to everyone else's and no matter what your GPA is, no matter how well you did in student teaching, and no matter how laudatory

---

1   Brisson, Tracy. *Confessions of a Teacher Recruiter: How to Create an Extraordinary Resume and Hook Your Dream Job* (San Bernardino, CA: The Opportunities Project, 2015).

your letters of recommendation may be – the harsh reality is that you'll never be the king of clubs, high on the hog, in like Flynn, or the whole nine yards (again, choose your own idiom). In short, you'll never be considered for a teaching position. Do what everyone else is doing (or not doing) and you will be one of many rather than *one of a kind.* Here's another way of putting it: Your resume and cover letter <u>must</u> distinguish you, in some positive way, from all the other candidates vying for the same position(s).

A TOUCH OF HUMOR

The following was actually included in one applicant's cover letter:
"Let's meet, so you can 'ooh' and 'aah' over my experience."

Getting a teaching position must be an active and systematic process. Doing what everyone else does (sending out endless batches of applications, correspondence, letters of recommendation, and resumes) will seldom guarantee you a job. Neither will using the same forms, models and templates everyone else is gathering from a college's career center. You need to set yourself apart from the crowd, you need to distinguish yourself as a candidate of promise, and you need to demonstrate initiative, drive, and enthusiasm. Above all, you must <u>sell yourself</u> as the most appropriate or most qualified candidate for an advertised position.

FROM THE PRINCIPAL'S DESK:

"Resumes that are brief, to the point, and highlight the candidate's potential impress me. I like to look for specific activities that show they are a well-rounded teaching candidate and able to handle the multitude of obligations expected of our teachers."

When I was in high school I was on the track team. My specialties were the 880 and mile (I was our school's only middle distance runner).

I particularly remember a home dual track meet we held on a sunny day in late April. We watched as the other team got off their bus and jogged into the locker room. A short time later several members of the opposing team came out and began to warm up on the track. However, one individual ambled over to a group of us and asked, "Who's your miler?" I identified myself and he came over, looked me square in the eye, and shook my hand. At the same time he said, "Hi, I'm Jeff, and I'm looking forward to beating your butt today!"

I wish I could report to you that, in stereotypical Hollywood fashion, I won (by mere inches) both our races (along with the usual crescendo of soaring violins, cascading cellos, and a stadium filled with thousands of wildly cheering fans), but such was not the case. He trounced me both times (in front of a crowd of 24 spectators). It was only afterwards that I figured out why – he had made a lasting first impression on me even before we had laced up our spikes and toed the start line. He had planted a potent seed in my head that had an effect on how well I was to run both races that day.

Resumes and cover letters are also <u>first impressions</u>. They will either clearly establish you as a contender for a posted position or they will identify you as just another candidate similar to every other candidate applying for the same position. In short, if you don't make a good first impression – if you don't plant a seed in the mind of the resume reader – you won't finish in first place (getting an interview). Someone else will win the race and you'll finish with the rest of the pack.

Your resume and cover letter must distinguish you, in some positive way, from all the other candidates vying for the same position(s).

This book contains all the information you need to write that winning resume and equally winning cover letter. I'll show you what commands the attention of busy administrators sifting through tall stacks of applications, the key words and phrases that highlight your qualifications and skills, and the formatting that will clearly establish you as an exciting and dynamic candidate – one any principal would love to interview. I've included plenty of sample resumes and cover letters, first-hand tips and strategies from elementary and secondary principals, and how to handle special situations. I'll also provide you with lots of inside information available in no other resource – information that will move you to the head of the class.

Several bonus features have also been sprinkled throughout the pages of this book. These include:

- **From The Principal's Desk** – For this book, I contacted scores of elementary, middle school, and secondary principals from around the United States. I sent out questionnaires, e-mailed surveys, conducted phone interviews, and scheduled numerous face-to-face interviews with experienced administrators from a wide variety of schools across the country. Their "words of wisdom" will give you inside information available nowhere else.

- **Insider Tip** – These sections include valuable "intelligence" from full-time recruiters, newly hired classroom teachers, school district administrators, and professional resume writers. You'll get inside information available in no other resource.

- **Extra Credit** – These are activities and exercises designed to give you an edge in writing your resume or your cover letter. Yes, these are "homework assignments" – but this is homework with a difference: helping you craft the best documents possible.

- **A Touch of Humor** – Over the year I spent writing this book I've been collecting quotes, statements, and "wisdom" from various resumes and cover letters that are…well…just a little unbelievable. None of these are made up – they are all direct excerpts from actual resumes and cover letters. It is my hope they will bring a smile to your face as they did to mine!

Over the course of more than four-and-a-half decades of teaching experience, service on a plethora of search committees, and work as a former program administrator I have read an amazing number of resumes and cover letters. Most were unmemorable, unexciting and frequently unprofessional. Far too many had been crafted with little attention to important details or the specifics of an advertised position. In a word, they were: ☑ lousy, ☑ terrible, ☑ awful, ☑ lame!

On the other hand, I've also read resumes that had me on the edge of my seat – resumes that made me want to bring in that candidate immediately for an interview. These were ones that grabbed my attention and never let go – resumes that clearly identified an educator who would make an absolute and clear difference in the lives of students. In some cases I hired people (at least in my mind) on nothing more than a one-page resume and a one-page cover letter.

I sincerely hope you will use my experiences along with the information I have gathered from school district administrators and other hiring professionals across the country to help you prepare your professional resume and equally professional cover letter. I know you'll find this information valuable whether you are anticipating your first teaching job or whether you are an experienced teacher looking for a change of venue. I promise you down-to-earth advice and a book overflowing with tips, strategies and techniques that will help you get that all-important interview.

Remember, writing a resume and cover letter is all about making an impression – a good first impression. Here's how to make yours the best!

Part I

Creating an A+ Resume

Chapter 1

What They Never Told You in College

On a recent vacation, my wife and I traveled to northern California to hike and explore the redwood forests of Redwoods National and State Parks. We were absolutely amazed at these arboreal giants – botanical kings that soared skyward in splendid groves tucked into deep valleys and along seldom-traveled byways. We often found ourselves hiking deep into fog-shrouded landscapes and multi-sensory ecosystems far from the cacophony of the "civilized world." We were wide-eyed explorers in a primeval world full of mystery and magic. Our minds and our cameras were crowded with splendid scenes of majestic trees that defied description, yet always amazed with their majesty and serenity.

I was there, in part, to conduct some research for a children's book (*Tall, Tall Tree* [Nevada City, CA: Dawn Publications, 2017]) I was writing about the abundance of animals that live high in the branches of these ancient landmarks.[1] In the course of talking with park rangers, wandering these dense forests, researching reams of publications, and communicating with noted scientific authorities I gathered an amazing amount of information about redwood trees – information I had previously been unaware of. For example:

- The first redwood fossils date back more than 200 million years to the Jurassic period (when the dinosaurs were around).

- These trees can live for more than 2,000 years. Several redwoods alive today were also living during the time of the Roman Empire.

- The world's tallest tree is a redwood in Redwoods National and State Park in northern California. It is 379.1 feet tall or nearly six stories taller than the Statue of Liberty.

---

1. It has been estimated that more than 60 species of mammals, 18 species of amphibians, 11 species of reptiles, untold numbers of invertebrates, and 280 bird species live in and around redwood forests.

- A single redwood tree may weigh up to four million pounds (about the weight of a Saturn 5 rocket).

- The width of a redwood trunk can be more than 27 feet (more than twice the height of a school bus).

- A 300-foot redwood tree transports approximately 500 gallons of water up its trunk each day.

The facts bulleted above have been verified and confirmed by numerous scientists and are indisputable. The same is true about resumes – they too, have some basic facts necessary to their "mission" (as we will learn later in this book). However, just like the diversity of creatures living high in the canopy of a 300-foot redwood tree, there are some facts about resumes that are hidden from view…facts you seldom hear about, but facts important to your success in obtaining an interview and, eventually, a teaching position.

The Hidden Facts

You will undoubtedly be amazed at some of these "facts in hiding" about resumes since they may contradict information you may have received from your college career center, from friends or professors, or from information you may have picked up on the web or in magazine articles. Knowing these principles ahead of time can save you from making classic resume blunders and give you a leg up on the competition you will be facing in securing the teaching job of your dreams.

Your resume is your most important document. In conversations with school administrators from around the country one fact became abundantly clear: Of all the documents you might submit to a school or district in response to an advertised job opening, it is the resume that is THE MOST IMPORTANT DOCUMENT. I purposely capitalized letters in the previous sentence to focus your attention on this critical and essential fact of life. There is a good chance that all of the other material in your application packet will go unread (initially) and that your resume will be the single document that will determine if you get considered for a future interview.

While the statement above may shock you, it's part of the reality of the job most administrators face every day. Selecting a new member of the faculty is just one of a plethora of responsibilities principals have to accomplish…and that's on top of all the other duties and tasks that take up major portions of their day. As a result, many principals have developed strategies that help them sort through an (often) enormous stack of applications – strategies that are both time-saving and efficient. Truth be told, most administrators have, over the term of their career, developed ways to quickly and easily read a resume to see if there is a match between a candidate and a job.

That's not to say that everything else in your application packet is unimportant. Those other documents will be used to supplement the information included on your resume. However, you must pass the "resume test" first. If you do, then the other items are "value added" documents. However, if you do not pass the "resume test" the other items are seldom, if ever, reviewed. Bottom line: Your resume is your most important document!

A TOUCH OF HUMOR

I may have thought this, but was never brave enough to include it (as did this applicant) on any of my resumes: "Seeking a party-time position with potential for advancement."

College career centers cater to every major. It's a numbers game! Depending on the size of your college, the career center may have to deal with hundreds, if not thousands, of soon-to-be graduates – each of whom has just finished a four-year program and each of whom is seeking to become gainfully employed. It's an overwhelming task, to be sure. You may be just one among all those hundreds or thousands of job seekers who would like some career advice. Your college's career center has to be all things to all people – setting up job fairs, assisting in writing application materials, providing mock interview sessions, or offering a plethora of printed materials. In most cases they are overworked and over-tasked. Equally important, they have to be sufficiently informed about each and every major on your campus and the job requirements of all those occupations on both a local and regional level. As a result, they may have a modicum of knowledge about some occupations and an abundance of background about others.

This is not a condemnation of college career centers; rather, it is a reality. In so many ways, they must be all things to all people. Are they worth your time? Absolutely! They can get you started on this incredible new journey of yours. They can answer your questions and steer you in the right direction. They can provide you with insights that you may not be able to obtain on your own. But, please don't make the mistake of assuming that they are your one and only resource. You need a variety of resources – such as this book – to help you in a very competitive (and often confusing) employment process, particularly in education. The fact that you have taken the initiative to obtain this book is a credit to your desire to succeed as a classroom teacher. It is also a realization that part of the reason for that success will come from you – your initiative to go "above and beyond" the "usual" (one or two quick visits to the career center) will help establish you as a teacher candidate worthy of serious consideration.

✓EXTRA CREDIT:

Most college career centers offer a wide variety of events throughout the academic year. These may include such things as career fairs, mock interviews, guest speakers discussing the interview process, "Meet and Greets," social events with school administrators, and the like. It would be to your advantage to attend as many of these as possible – not just in your senior year, but throughout your academic career. You'll get lots of useful information from a wide variety of sources. Most important, you'll become very comfortable with various aspects of the application process ensuring your success when you actually do it on your own.

Not all college career centers are created equal. I sincerely hope you attend a college that has a viable, thorough, and engaging Career Center – one that is truly looking out for your interests in a very competitive job market. However, as you might expect, not all College Career Centers are created equal. Some are excellent, some are good, some are marginal, and some are…well, let's just say that some are barely worth your time.

In my research for this book I contacted many college career centers across the country. One of the items I was most interested in reviewing was each institution's "Resume Writing and Cover Letter Tips" for soon-to-graduate Education majors. What I discovered were documents that ranged from "Extremely Informative and Helpful" to "????????"... and everything in between. I was most concerned with those student documents that were inaccurate, incomplete, and, at times, unacceptable. Here are a few examples:

A.

From one college comes a 19-page document entitled "Teacher Resume Writing Booklet." In the brief section on cover letters they provide the following "Sample Cover Letter" (just the 1st paragraph is duplicated below):

Dear _____:

This letter of application is in regard to the entry level position with State Farm Insurance Companies. On May 19, _____, I will receive my Bachelor of Arts degree in Accounting. I am very interested in obtaining a position with your company. I believe that my qualifications well match those of the accounting position.

I think it would have been slightly more helpful to include a sample cover letter (in the *Teacher Resume Writing Booklet*) that classroom teachers (not accountants) would actually be able to use. In addition, this introductory paragraph is stale, hackneyed, and would never get any kind of favorable response. (See Chapter 19 in this book.)

B.

The Career Center at another college has a 7-page document entitled "Resume Writing Basics for Teachers." In one of the two sample resumes included, the following information (slightly shortened) was used as an example under "Professional Preparation":

Scheduled meetings with the principal. Teach lessons in spelling, math, reading, and vocabulary. Plan lessons for a small reading group. Created and oversaw a center activity every week. Attend SST meetings and team meetings. Meet and work with student's parents. Conferenced with parents on student's progress.

This example suffers on two fronts: 1) There is a mix of verb tenses – past tense (*scheduled, created*) along with present tense (*plan, meet*). 2) The apostrophe in "student's" is misplaced (The author isn't referring to a single student's parents, but all students.). This resume, I can assure you, would get tossed by most administrators simply because of those spelling and grammatical errors. (See Chapter 12 in this book.)

C.

A major university provides its students with a 6-page document entitled "A Teacher's Resume." As part of a 3-page sample resume the following information is included in the section entitled "Work Experience":

_____ ***Candies, Inc.,*** *Virginia Beach, VA*

Place orders for store merchandise and candy
Develop weekly schedules
Train new employees
Manage weekly inventory
Maintain weekly sales journal
Assist customers with purchases

C. (cont.)

Teacher resumes should only contain information related to teaching. Jobs and volunteer experiences that do not directly involve youngsters should not be included on a teaching resume. Working as a counselor at a summer camp is appropriate to include; selling candy to tourists is not. (See Chapter 5 in this book.) Also, a 3-page resume is way too long for a soon-to-be college graduate. One to one-and-a-quarter pages is quite enough. (See Chapter 12 in this book.)

It should be evident that there is some misinformation disseminated on a few college campuses. That's not to condemn ALL college career centers, but rather to illustrate that some of the information out there may not be the best. Most colleges provide their students with appropriate career counseling services, information, and timely documents. Others – not so much.

First impressions do count! I recently attended a Teacher Recruitment Fair – one held every spring in our local area. Over five dozen school district recruiters from across the country (in addition to two from Sweden) were there to offer teaching positions to more than 550 soon-to-be college graduates from eleven different colleges. As I walked around and visited with recruiters, I asked many of them to offer a critical piece of advice every potential teacher should consider when drafting a resume or cover letter. Almost every one of them told me something like, "I have a limited amount of time to read resumes, so remember that first impressions count!"

FROM THE PRINCIPAL'S DESK:

"Believe it or not, first impressions DO count. The resume should be clearly designed and easy to read."

As you will discover in Chapter 2, recruiters devote a very short amount of time with each and every resume. You can help them get the most information in the shortest amount of time possible by designing your document so that most of it can be read quickly and efficiently. No one will read your entire resume during an initial screening process so it is vitally important that its design be clear, simple, and clean. Keep the reader in mind – the question shouldn't be "How can I present myself in the best way?", but rather, "How can I help the reader learn why I'm the best qualified for the position – in the most effective way possible?"

Principals don't read every item on your resume. Every building principal has numerous and non-stop responsibilities. They must handle a whirlwind of duties, demands, schedules, unexpected events, and last minute chores that strain their patience and their resolve. It's like a circus performer who juggles fifteen bowling balls while encouraging a dozen lions to jump through flaming hoops AND walking a tightrope a hundred feet in the air. And, that's every day. To say that principals are overworked and overscheduled would be to understate the obvious.

With their time so precious it is not unusual for many administrators to have developed a series of time-saving techniques and strategies that help them wade through an, oftentimes, towering stack of job applications. Over the years, they have learned various signs and signals that identify those resumes that are less than professional, as well as those signs and signals that designate resumes that are the "cream of the crop." As a result, it is not necessary to read every single item on every single resume to know which ones are outstanding and which ones will be deposited in the nearest "circular file." You'll learn more about how this is done in Chapter 2.

Your resume is not a summary of your life. Here are descriptions written by two separate individuals. Based solely on these brief overviews, which person do you think principals would be most interested in meeting?

A.

– "I have been interested in computers ever since I was in third grade. When I was in high school I was the vice-president of the Cedarville Computer Club. I learned a lot about computers there. When I went to college I was able to work on a really cool computer program. It was a very successful program used by many people on campus."

B.

– "Developed and designed an innovative app matching singles across campus. After a 3-month trial run, assessment data revealed a 23% increase in the number of confirmed dates visiting Murph's Study Hall (the local student hangout) on Saturday evenings."

Not surprisingly, most principals would select Person B. That's simply because B provides readers with a "product" to sell. She or he marketed herself or himself by appealing to a basic need. Person A, on the other hand, just described something about herself or himself. That individual simply shared some personal information. She or he was not particularly interested in what the reader wanted or what a principal may have been looking for. They simply related some events from their past. In short, not very exciting stuff!

Here's one of the most critical features you need to know about a well-constructed resume: it must be designed to <u>sell</u> you, not <u>tell everything</u> about you. We'll spend more time on this critical concept in a later chapter (Chapter 3).

A TOUCH OF HUMOR

One applicant included the following on her resume: "Achievements: Nominated for prom queen."

Good Resumes Tell Stories

From the earliest of times, humans have always enjoyed good stories (remember, these were the times before Facebook and Twitter). In many civilizations and cultures professional storytellers were revered and praised and it was quite the social event to have one of these professionals wander into a village and share his tales of imaginary animals, great battles, or fantastical kingdoms. These stories were both compelling and memorable.

Most people make the unfortunate mistake of assuming that a resume is merely a listing of the things one has done in all her or his previous jobs. Not so! A good resume is one that tells a story. After all, would you rather have someone read you a list of all the different pairs of shoes a popular singer has or would you rather hear a story about a day in the life of a popular singer? So it is with resumes – you can capture (and keep) the attention of a busy school administrator much better with a series of stories than you can with a listing of accomplishments.

In most cases, a typical resume is a bland recitation of standardized phrases and common descriptions – nothing that grabs (and holds) the attention of a reader. These documents are simple and straightforward listings – there is no representation of the vibrant, exciting, or energetic human being who wrote about those events. On the other hand, a resume of stories sets you apart from the crowd – it adds personality to your document and makes you memorable.

> **Fact:** "Was responsible for teaching social studies lessons and assessing students."
>
> **Story:** "Designed and taught an inquiry-based/ hands-on social studies unit focused on 'Time and Timekeeping' which has now been incorporated into the overall sixth grade curriculum. End-of-year assessments indicated a 17% improvement over the previous year's scores in social studies."

Stories also have the advantage of creating images in the minds of readers or listeners. It is those images that make a story memorable. Think about some of your courses. The ones you enjoyed most were those that offered up stories, anecdotes, or vignettes about various topics. The courses you liked the least were those that focused, almost entirely, on the memorization of facts, data, and (apparently useless) bits of information.

You have another "resume" in the works. This might be a good time to turn to Appendix A at the back of this book and read those pages in their entirety. Before you put your formal resume together, you should be aware of your "hidden resume" and what it means for your job chances. Please don't ignore the importance of this information.

You are more similar than you are different. Here's a harsh dose of reality: You and everyone else who applies for a specific teaching position look more alike than you do different. In other words, to a principal, you and the other applicants all look fairly similar. Let's take a look:

- All the applicants (either elementary, middle school, or secondary), irrespective of the college or university they attended took, pretty much, the same courses. The titles of those courses may have been slightly different, but the content was, for the most part, fairly similar. For example, I teach a course every semester entitled "Teaching Elementary Science" – a course designed for Elementary Education majors. Even though you may have attended a completely different institution in another state, the chances are pretty good that if your certification will be in Elementary Education, you too, have taken a course on teaching science (e.g. "Principles of Elementary Science," "Elementary Science: Principles and Practices," etc.). The same thing holds true for all your other methods courses.

- All the applicants for a specific teaching position will have achieved a GPA within a very narrow range. For the most part, most of the GPAs will be somewhere between 3.0 and 4.0 (A recent study conducted at the University of Maine showed that the average cumulative GPA of all teacher candidates – elementary, secondary, special education – graduating over a five-year period ranged between 3.25 and 3.70.).

- All the applicants have completed a student teaching experience (or experiences) successfully. They have all designed and developed lesson plans, they've all dealt with student behavior issues in the classroom, they've all conferred with their cooperating teachers on numerous occasions, and they all have graded innumerable exams, papers, and homework assignments. And they all have achieved a high grade for their student teaching assignment.

- All the applicants will submit glowing, laudatory, celebratory, praising, and congratulatory letters of recommendation. After all, you don't ask someone to write a letter of recommendation unless you are sure that individual is going to write an incredibly positive and delightfully upbeat document about your teaching prowess.

FROM THE PRINCIPAL'S DESK:

"Everyone comes in with the same experiences. What have you done outside your regular studies?"

So, (you may be asking yourself) how do I stand out if every one of the candidates (myself included) seems to be more similar than different? How do I rise above the fray and get a teaching interview? Those are excellent questions and ones we'll answer in succeeding chapters. Know, however, that the specific content and form of your application documents (such as a resume and cover letter) can give you a decided and distinguished advantage over your competition.

There is no such thing as a perfect resume. In researching the topic of this book I contacted numerous principals around the country, talked with professional recruiters in many different school districts, consulted with college career centers at several institutions, and did some extensive reading in a number of journals and books seeking the best advice for soon-to-be teachers (such as yourself) getting ready to enter the job market. As you might expect, I gathered a considerable amount of data regarding the design and data necessary in a well-constructed resume. But, what I didn't find was a universal consensus of what each and every resume should have. That is to say, there is no such thing as an all-purpose, universally precise, and singular resume that will satisfy everyone. What you will discover in the pages of this book is a series of recommendations and suggestions from some of the best minds in the country. What you won't find (sorry) is the perfect, ideal, no-fault resume that will guarantee you an automatic invitation to come in for an interview with every school district you apply to. Such a document just doesn't exist.

A TOUCH OF HUMOR

"I was hiring high school teachers when I encountered a resume that included 'torturing middle school students' in its Experience section."

I don't want you to be discouraged by the previous paragraph. That's because perfection is an ideal, it's never a goal. Allow me to share an example. Over the course of my teaching career I've been privileged to write a considerable number of books. These include teacher resource books, college textbooks, children's books, and several adult non-fiction titles. The book you're now holding in your hands is my 153rd published book. As part of my writing ventures I have been invited as a visiting author in many schools around the country, in addition to leading several writing workshops at conferences and other literary events. One of the questions I'm sometimes asked at those events is, "If you could, are there any of your books you would want to revise or improve?" My response is always the same – "Yes, all of them!" That's because there's no such thing as a perfect book. After a book has been released I may learn new things about the topic. I talk to new people and get some new information. I see sentences and paragraphs that could be restructured or re-formatted. I see a different organizational plan or an alternate emphasis. In my conversations with other professional writers they often say the same thing. All pieces of writing can be improved because writing, like education, is always evolutionary. ...it's always a process; seldom a product. As a result, the perfect resume doesn't exist. Please don't make that your goal. Rather, your goal should be to create a resume that presents you as an extremely qualified applicant for a specified teaching position.

* * *

That said, please know that this book will provide you with time-tested and proven techniques to grab the attention of very busy administrators. You'll learn about elements of resumes that eliminate most teacher candidates from any further consideration. You'll discover factors that will focus positively on the qualities and attributes principals are looking for in new staff members. And, most important, you'll be able to put yourself in the best light possible – a light that will positively illuminate your qualities, attitudes, and potential contributions to any school. You'll shine simply because you'll be able to do what few others will – *Ace Your Teacher Resume (and Cover Letter)*!

Chapter 2

You Only Have Six Seconds

I'm going to start this chapter by giving you a test. Not a difficult test, but a test nonetheless. Below this paragraph are two boxes – labeled "A" and "B." Each box contains the start of a story (neither story is complete). I'd like to invite you to read the incomplete story in each box and then answer the question underneath the two boxes. Ready? Go.

A.

Los Angeles is located in southern California. It is the largest city in the state. It was founded in 1781. Four million people live in Los Angeles. Its nickname is

---

B.

Tears streamed down her face. It was the happiest day of her life. A sparkling diamond! A real true-to-life diamond was on her finger. Tenderly, she looked up

---

Each story was written by a different author. Which author would you be most interested in meeting?

❏ Author "A"

❏ Author "B"

If you are like most people who take this "test," you will have selected author "B" as the one you would most like to meet. What makes that a most interesting decision is that you were able to select your "favorite" author in just six seconds. That's right – six seconds. Let's take a look.

The average adult reader in the United States reads at a rate of approximately 300 words per minute. That works out to about five words per second (300 words per minute divided by 60 seconds = 5 words per second). Count the number of words in each of the two boxes above and you'll note that there are exactly 30 words in each box. If you are an average reader (5 words per second), then it took you about six seconds to read all the words in box "A" and another six seconds to read all the words in box "B." Based on those two six-second frames of reading time you were able to make a determination as to which author might be the most interesting to meet.

Six seconds!

FROM THE PRINCIPAL'S DESK:

"Everyone comes in with the same experiences. "I only have so much time. Make sure your resume is easy to read with a simple format."

What Resume Readers Actually Do

In 2012 an extensive and exhaustive research study[1] was conducted to assess recruiter's on-the-job behavior. This ground-breaking research employed a scientific technique called "eye tracking" – a technologically advanced assessment of eye movement that records and analyzes where and how long a person focuses when digesting information or completing activities. The study gauged specific behaviors of actual recruiters as they performed various tasks, including resume and candidate profile reviews. Thirty professional recruiters took part in the study during a 10-week period.

Some of the most surprising findings from the study involved the fundamentals of the recruiter's resume review process. For example, and despite recruiter's different self-reports, the study found that recruiters **spend only six seconds reviewing an individual resume** – irrespective of the actual length of the resume.

---

1 *Eye Tracking Online Metacognition: Cognitive Complexity and Recruiter Decision Making.* Will Evans, Head of User Experience Design, TheLadders, 2012.

In addition, the "gaze tracking" technology showed that recruiters spent almost 80% of their resume review time on the following data points: Name, Current Position: Title, Institution, Dates, Previous Position: Title, Institution, Dates, and Education. Beyond these data points, recruiters did little more than scan for keywords to match an open position, which amounted to a very cursory "pattern matching" activity. Because decisions were based mostly on the data listed above, an individual's resume detail and explanatory copy had little to no impact on **the initial decision making**. In fact, the study's eye tracking technology also showed that recruiters spent about **six seconds** on their initial "fit/no fit" decision.

Six seconds!

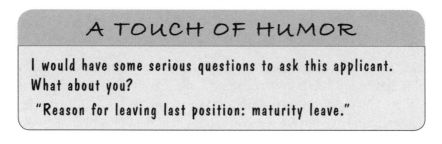

A TOUCH OF HUMOR

I would have some serious questions to ask this applicant. What about you?

"Reason for leaving last position: maturity leave."

Does this mean you should only be concerned with the first 30 words of your resume? Well, yes…and no. Let's take a look.

A few years ago, one of the schools in the county where I live and work advertised for an elementary teaching position. The position was open for just one week. By the end of the week a total of 404 applications had been received by the building principal. To say that his initial task – wading through this ocean of applications – was enormous would be to understate the obvious. It was equally obvious that he needed to pare down the stack of applicants to a precious few. How much time (on average) do you think he spent with each of those 404 resumes? That's right – about six seconds each. In those six seconds he was able to make the same kind of decisions you made earlier in this chapter with the two reading samples ("A" and "B"). In each case, his job was simple: Is this candidate an "accept" or "reject"?

By the time he was finished with that first run-through he had less than 50 applications on his desk. Now, he could go back and read each of the remaining resumes again; but, this time, in somewhat more detail (and with more time).

FROM THE PRINCIPAL'S DESK:

"What I like to see is a succinct resume that is easy/clear to read. I don't have time to read through a lot of information. At the same time, I do not want to have to search for relevant information, and I want it clearly presented. The formatting is important. When I see a resume with these things, it makes me want to look over it in greater detail."

But, here's the critical point. It's not the first 30 words of your resume that makes the difference (as opposed to the first 30 words in the story in box "A" and the first 30 words in the story in box "B.") The eye-tracking research study enumerated above showed that the 30 words a recruiter focused on were systematically "selected" based upon established designs and formats of professional resumes. In other words, it's not the first 30 words – but rather a select 30 words (as determined by the recruiter's eyes). What this means for you is that all your words must be pertinent, descriptive, specific and explanatory. You don't know for certain which 30 words a principal might focus on, so you need to be sure all your words are worthy of being included in that 30-word "eye review" process. By the same token, time spent on every word in a resume will also ensure that after a successful initial review by a principal, those same words will now be read with considerably more attention in the more thorough follow-up review.

INSIDER TIP

Bullets "command" a reader's eyes to focus on the word or words following that graphic symbol. That's why (as you will learn in Chapters 3 and 8) it is important to have a powerful verb (usually in the past tense) following each bulleted item on your resume. For example:

Weak:
I helped my cooperating teacher....

Strong:
Developed and implemented an integrated unit....

Six seconds. That's not much time for a big decision. But, it can be the most important six seconds of your career. Spend the time crafting a resume that gets positive attention in its first read-through – as well as a followup read-through – and you could wind up with the job of your dreams.

INSIDER TIP

What happens in six seconds?
- 450 McDonald's hamburgers are sold.
- 2,100 pizza slices are eaten in the U.S.
- 27,600 tweets are posted.
- 246,000 Facebook posts are posted.
- 20,000,000+ emails are sent.
- 600 lightning strikes hit the earth.
- 9,000 bottles of water are consumed in the U.S.
- More than 42,000 Coca-Cola products are consumed.
- About 25 babies are born in the world.
- About 10 people die in the world.
- 95,017 pounds of trash are thrown away in the U.S.
- 96 million tons of water evaporate from the earth's surface.
- Amazon sells more than $8000.00 worth of products.
- A single resume is read!

Chapter 3

Sell, Don't Tell!

In my conversations with professional recruiters, school district administrators, and college career counselors throughout the country, one critical piece of advice kept coming up again and again. Here it is:

A job search is all about marketing.

The bottom line in any job search is that you are trying to sell yourself – more specifically, you are trying to sell someone on the benefits of **you** and the benefits you will bring to a school or school district. In short, you are the product. Just like a flashy new car, the latest and greatest technological innovation, or a newly released drug designed to eradicate specific pain and suffering, you are a product. Someone could tell me about all the features on that new car, but that wouldn't inspire me to want to purchase the car. What they need to do is sell me on all those new features…why do I need those specific features on that specific car? When they do that they're trying to sell me the car.

FROM THE PRINCIPAL'S DESK:
"Stand out in a positive way. Make yourself unique in a positive way."

Professional resume writers will tell you that the single-most important feature they include in every single resume they write is the "Sell, Don't Tell" strategy. When you "tell it" you are simply stating basic facts ("I taught fourth grade science."). On the other hand, when you "sell it" you are drawing attention to it, you are advertising it, you are promoting it, and you are underlining its importance to the consumer ("Initiated and developed an inquiry-based life science curriculum for fourth grade students – one that resulted in an 11% gain in standardized test scores.").

Master resume writers will tell you that the "Sell, don't tell" strategy should be woven into every single item included on a well-written resume. Ignore it and your resume will sound like every other resume.

Let's look at the difference:

Tell it	Sell it
"Taught four sections of chemistry during student teaching."	"Designed and produced a revision to the 10th grade chemistry curriculum that resulted in heighted awareness of chemistry in everyday activities along with a 17% improvement in overall attitudes towards chemistry."
"Tutored a child."	"Tutored special needs child in reading and writing resulting in an increased reading level of two grades."
"Read stories to children at the public library."	"Set up and ran a Saturday morning read-aloud club at the local library which resulted in a 19% increase in attendance of patrons over the length of the project."
"Was a volunteer coach for the junior varsity soccer team."	"Established a physical fitness program for junior varsity soccer players that resulted in a significant decrease in athletic injuries and a heighted awareness of sustained conditioning exercises."
"Taught high school math."	"Instructed algebra, geometry, and pre-calculus students in grades 9-11. Developed and implemented appropriate lesson plans and assessments to meet state standards, resulting in a 93% advanced or proficient rating in 11th grade PSSA."
"Wrote a new social studies unit."	"Researched and designed an interactive unit on the Underground Railroad that resulted in improved attitudes about the role of African Americans in U.S. history along with a statistically significant improvement in student mid-term grades."

As you review the chart opposite, you can see that "selling" yourself (as opposed to "telling" yourself) results in slightly longer statements. Does that mean some more work for you? You bet! But, with the "Sell, don't tell" philosophy you are putting your best features "front and center." Any reader will get a clearer picture of just who you are. Check out the difference in the following chart:

Telling it	**Selling it**
Details activities	Details your activities + includes the results of those activities.
Describes features.	Describes your features + also provides the benefits of those features.
Focuses on what was done.	Focuses on what you did + how what you did benefitted teachers, administrators, or students.
Tells what and how.	Sells the "what" + sells the "how" + sells why those two elements are significant.

A TOUCH OF HUMOR

One applicant's resume included the following under Skills: "Can function without additional oxygen at 24,000 feet."

The A-1 Resume

I'd like to take you through an exercise I've used to help undergraduate students understand what a resume should really do. As emphasized throughout this book, resumes are not a collection of facts related to your education, teaching experience, and/or work history. Resumes should not be *reports* on you, but rather should be *advertisements* about you. As emphasized in the section above, attention-grabbing resumes are designed to sell, not tell.

Imagine, for a moment, that you wanted to bring a bottle of steak sauce to someone's attention. You could do what I sometimes ask students to do and write a "resume" for that bottle of steak sauce. Here is an example of a "resume" submitted by one student:

A-1 Steak Sauce
Kraft Foods Group, Inc.
Northfield, IL 60093-2753

Objective: Condiment for meat

Ingredients include tomato puree, vinegar, corn syrup, salt, and raisin paste (among others). Can also be used on steak, pork and chicken. Has approximately 17 servings in a 10-oz bottle and is manufactured by Kraft Foods.

Areas of Proficiency:

- Has 3 grams of carbohydrates in an average serving
- Has 0 grams of fat in each serving
- Has 280 mg of salt in each tablespoon
- Has 15 calories per tablespoon

Education & Qualifications

Bachelor of Culinary Arts (1831); Major: Food Accessories

United Kingdom University, London, England

Professional Experiences

The Smith Household – Carbondale, CO 1995 – Present

Condiment

Was a condiment for a family of five. Helped to flavor their steaks and chicken dishes. Met their dietary needs. Had a permanent place in the family refrigerator. Appeared many times on the weekly shopping list.

Steak and Suds Restaurant – Indianapolis, IN 1980 – Present

Table condiment

Was included on every table. A feature at every meal. Accompanied salt and pepper shakers. Stood next to mustard and ketchup bottles. Frequently used by patrons.

Achievements:

- Have been used in thousands of dishes across the country.
- A "personality" in several TV commercials.
- Tastes really good.
- Easily recognized in grocery stores throughout the U.S.
- Distinctive bottle shape.

Professional Contributions

Member, Kraft Foods family of products

Member, Products with Their Own Web Site

As you will note from the "resume" above, it is simply a collection of facts easily obtained from the label on a bottle of *A-1 Sauce* as well as information from the Wikipedia entry for *A-1 Sauce*. This resume simply tells you about *A-1 Sauce* – it tells you about its ingredients, it tells you when it was first created, it tells you where it can be found, it tells you how it could be used, and it tells you some of its most basic information.

What it doesn't do is: sell!

FROM THE PRINCIPAL'S DESK:

"Most resumes appear formatted the same way so when reviewing so many they tend to blend together. I believe that your resume can reflect your personality or character traits so wording is an important message to convey."

Now, just for fun, let's take that same bottle of *A-1 Sauce* and write a "selling" resume – a resume that sets it apart from other condiments and one that highlights its talents and attributes for a potential buyer. Here's how it might look:

A-1 Steak Sauce
Kraft Foods Group, Inc.
Northfield, IL 60093-2753

Objective: Condiment for meat

Dedicated food enhancement with a long-standing reputation among discriminating chefs. In addition, is an accommodating and versatile sauce with the talent to enhance a wide variety of meats. Demonstrated ability to be flexible, ensuring that every diner's tastes are addressed. Moreover, superior ingredients and flavoring skills are designed to foster a rich and delicious culinary experience.

Areas of Proficiency:

- Creative meal preparation
- Manufactured to help every cook succeed
- Multifunctional flavoring for every diner
- Unique integration of spices
- Formulated for culinary success

Education & Qualifications

Bachelor of Culinary Arts (1831); Major: Food Accessories
United Kingdom University, London, England

Professional Experiences

The Smith Household – Carbondale, CO 1995 – Present
Condiment

Primary sauce for a wide variety of dishes, met the culinary, epicurean, and gourmet tastes of a family of five for more than 20 years, served at informal get-togethers as well as formal dinner parties. Complimented an eclectic array of foods and garnered accolades from both adults and children.

Steak and Suds Restaurant – Indianapolis, IN 1980 – Present
Table condiment

Enhanced numerous dishes and was instrumental in the design and creation of unique recipes – winning several prestigious awards (e.g. 2016 La Société de Sauce Gold Medal). Endorsed by patrons as an ideal complement for pork, beef, chicken, and fish; universal compliment to an eclectic assembly of menu items.

Achievements:

- Supported a delicious array of family dinners through the inclusion of unique and distinctive spices.
- Integrated a rich and satisfying condiment into the culinary experiences of millions of Americans.
- Employed olfactory, visual, and gustatory senses to make dinners more interesting and sensual.
- Enhanced the dining experience by using varied spices, vegetables, and fruits in a savory arrangement; included a unique arrangement of vinegar, tomato puree and dried onions to provide an exceptional eating experience and positive culinary attitudes.
- Fostered a sense of epicurean curiosity and a deeper appreciation for unique condiments in any dining experience.

Professional Contributions

Active Participant, Kraft Foods family of products
Founding Member, International Condiments Consortium
Distinguished Member, Meatloaf Institute
Honorary Member, Backyard Barbeque Association

Do you see the difference? In this "resume," the value to the reader is emphasized moreso than the facts and figures of the individual (or the product). This is a "selling" resume – one designed to make you want to know more about the individual (or product) behind that resume. I would hope that the second resume would be much more encouraging (than the first one) in making you want to go out and purchase a bottle of *A-1 Sauce*. If it does, then it does the same thing you want your resume to do – to **sell** a very busy principal on you…to **sell** her or him on the idea that you should be brought in for an interview…and to **sell** her or him on the thought that you should be the one she or he offers a teaching position.

Bottom line: You'll get more positive responses (from principals) with a resume that **sells**, than you ever will with a resume that **tells**. Or, look at it this way: A good resume is all about selling a story; a bad resume is all about telling the facts.

FROM THE PRINCIPAL'S DESK:

"All candidates must be able to sell themselves. In the past, I have always been sold and have always looked favorably on candidates who list experiences (in any capacity) working with children."

✓EXTRA CREDIT:

Here's an activity I've used with my students. You may want to do this yourself to get some important and necessary practice in writing a compelling and attention-grabbing resume.

1. Go to your local grocery store, or reach inside the pantry in your kitchen at home, and grab some sort of inanimate food object. Here are a few suggestions: a box of cereal, a jar of pickles, a can of tomatoes, a jar of peanut butter, a box of rice, a can of soup, a bottle of mustard, or a package of dried beans.

2. Pretend you are going to introduce that inanimate object to someone who has never experienced it before (perhaps someone new to this country or someone who has lived in a cabin deep in the woods all his life [a hermit]).

Chapter 4

Homework Assignment: Self-Inventory

Kelly Jacobson wanted to be a teacher ever since she was six years old. When it came time to choose a college she knew that Kroy College would be the perfect place. Kroy College had a reputation for a demanding and challenging teacher education program, – one that was celebrated by school administrators as educating pre-service teachers with both a breadth and depth of preparation. The college's reputation ensured that graduates were not only prepared for the challenges of classroom work, but that they were highly regarded by principals throughout the region as highly qualified applicants.

As Kelly began her student teaching experience in Mrs. March's fifth grade classroom, she knew she would have to begin work on her teaching resume…but where would she start? She had taken the same courses as all the other student teachers, had participated in similar field experiences during the past 3½ years, achieved high marks on most of her assignments, and knew that she would get excellent letters of recommendation from her professors and other education professionals with whom she had worked over the years.

But, what would she say on her resume? How could she make her resume stand out from all the others?

One afternoon, on her way home from a tough day of student teaching, she stopped by the supermarket to pick up some groceries for her and her two roommates. Salad dressing was one of the items on her list. As she stood in front of the expansive section of salad dressings, she was suddenly hit with a thought. "Wow, there are more than 100 different kinds of salad dressings here – different flavors, different brands, different shapes and sizes of bottles, different colors and label designs, and loads of different ingredients. How can anybody make a choice with all these selections?" Then it struck her – "How can a principal make a choice between so many different applicants for a teaching position? What do they look for? How do they separate the good ones from the not so good ones? How do they finalize their choices? How do they ever make a selection?"

What quickly became apparent to Kelly was the fact that school administrators are like supermarket shoppers. They are presented with an array of choices (salad dressings & teacher candidates) from which they must select the best one (best salad dressing & best teacher). As she began searching for the right dressing for the Black Bean and Couscous salad she was going to prepare that night, she also began thinking about the qualities and "ingredients" she had that might distinguish her from every other applicant – the right mix of features that might lead to an interview and an eventual teaching position.

On the advice of one of her professors, Kelly sat down one Saturday afternoon and began to list her "ingredients" – those skills that made her unique (and delicious) in the eyes of a potential employer. She recalled an "Introduction to Advertising" course one of her roommates had taken in her freshman year. She remembered her roommate mentioning three basic categories into which skills could be grouped:

Skills learned through past jobs, positions, and training (Experiences & Accomplishments)

Skills that demonstrate initiative, difference, uniqueness ("Added Value" Skills)

Personal traits and habits (Personality)

Kelly took a sheet of paper and turned it sideways. She then divided it into three individual columns. She spent the next two days adding words and phrases to each of the three columns. Here's part of what she wrote:

Experiences & Accomplishments	"Added Value" Skills	Personality
• Developed weekly progress reports for parents. • Participant in third grade team meetings. • Developed science thematic units for "Wild Animals" and "Oceans and Seas." • Taught full range of exceptional students. • Charged with maintaining "running records' for group of five students. • Integrated children's literature into two phases of social studies curriculum. • Achieved 91% passing rate on state reading exams.	• Volunteered at several community agencies. • Tutored child in reading. • Helped run student newspaper. • Assistant coach for JV basketball team. • Wrote articles for PTO newsletter. • Worked one-on-one with autistic child during student teaching. • Conferred with parents on homework policy.	• Good sense of humor • Creative • Friendly • Quick learner • Flexible • Independent • Well-organized • Good judgement

Kelly was smart – she didn't try to do this chart all on her own. Just as she got advice from her roommates on the kinds of salad dressings they preferred, she also solicited perceptions and observations from others in creating her list. She asked former professors, several classmates, her cooperating teacher and college supervisor, and even her best friend back home in Tucson, Arizona for the qualities and skills they saw in Kelly. She asked several people who knew her best to share their honest perceptions and appraisals – both professional as well as personal traits. As long as those suggestions were "education-related" Kelly included them on her initial draft of the chart.

Kelly kept the chart (an ever-evolving document) with her throughout her student teaching experience. She frequently added new items, subtracted other items, and modified entries until she felt that she had a true representation of who she was as both a (potential) classroom teacher and member of an education team.

Now she had the necessary ingredients she needed to write her resume.

But, But, But....

After reading the previous section, you're probably saying something like, "But, Doc, you're asking me to do more work. You're suggesting I write something **IN ADDITION TO** a resume! Are you crazy or what?"

Well, I can't answer that last question (although I'm sure many of my former students could!). But, you're right – I am suggesting that you take some time and draft your own self-inventory of skills. Yes, it's extra work – but, in doing so, you will be crafting an important foundation for the development of a solid, attention-getting resume – one that will help you stand out from the crowd and secure you a job interview. Sure, you could probably write your resume without going through this extra step of developing a self-inventory of skills. But, why not give yourself an opportunity to move ahead of the completion and distinguish yourself as a candidate of both merit and promise?

I know you're not a bottle of salad dressing, but remember what I shared in the previous chapter – you are your own best advertising agency. You certainly want to promote yourself in the best possible way...and you certainly want to "sell" yourself as the best possible teacher candidate applying for a specific position. A self-inventory is a great way to ensure those possibilities.

FROM THE PRINCIPAL'S DESK:

"Highlight what makes you rise above the many other candidates with a teaching degree. Keep the resume concise and clearly presented."

An Alternate Strategy

Anna Mae Lincoln was having a terrific student teaching experience in Mrs. Wallace's Biology classes. She had been given several responsibilities over the first few weeks of student teaching and by the sixth week of the experience, her cooperating teacher had sufficient trust in Anna Mae for her to take over all the Biology classes. It meant a lot more work for Anna Mae because now she was the one who had to create all the lesson plans, teach all the lessons, and assess all the students. But, she loved it!

It was about five weeks before graduation and Anna Mae had heard about two Biology positions opening up in a district near where she lived. One weekend she sat down in her apartment and began to assemble materials she could use for her resume and cover letter. One of the documents she pulled from her files was a list of the essential qualities of good teachers – a list she had obtained from one of her professors at Paymore State College. She knew that part of the "job" of the resume was to show how her qualifications matched the needs of a school or district. So, she decided to modify the list a little so she could assess her specific qualifications. She developed the following form:

Qualifications	
1. An engaging and enthusiastic personality	
2. A passion for teaching	
3. Establishes and maintains high behavioral expectations	
4. Engages students in their lessons	
5. Thorough knowledge of curriculum and standards	
6. Plans that ensure academic achievement	
7. Sets high academic expectations	
8. Structures and delivers well-crafted lessons	
9. Engages students in all lessons	
10. Integrates technology into lessons systematically	
11. Develops and maintains positive relationships with all students	
12. Addresses the diverse needs of all students	
13. Provides helpful and timely feedback	
14. Engages students in critical thinking	
15. Creates a strong classroom culture	
16. Works in collaboration with other educators	

Self Rating	My Personal Statement
5 ④ 3 2 1	I am totally committed to teaching and display that enthusiasm every day.
5 4 3 2 1	
5 4 3 2 1	
⑤ 4 3 2 1	Students are offered a wide variety of hands-on, minds-on activities.
5 4 3 2 1	
5 4 3 2 1	
5 4 3 2 1	
5 4 3 2 1	
5 4 3 2 1	
5 4 3 2 1	
⑤ 4 3 2 1	Know all student names and greet each one prior to every class.
5 4 3 2 1	
5 4 3 2 1	
5 ④ 3 2 1	Focus on high level cognitive questions that move students beyond simple recall.
5 4 3 2 1	
⑤ 4 3 2 1	Attend all department meetings and make active contributions to the discussions.

Anna Mae began to fill in the form. She knew it would take some time – time away from grading an ever-growing stack of student papers – but she also knew that she could not write an effective resume without knowing specifically her strengths and how she could best present those strengths to a prospective principal. She felt it would be time well spent.

Anna Mae discovered that this exercise made it much easier for her to design and develop a list of specific experiences that could be bulleted on her resume (see the following chapter). The exercise also alerted her to some of the items she would need to attend to during the last few weeks of her student teaching experience. In so doing, she also was generating some interesting discussion points about how she was working toward becoming a better teacher – a fact particularly important to share during any forthcoming job interviews.

Yes, this was a lot of work. But you, too, can profit from this exercise as much as Anna Mae did. Duplicate the chart on the next page and fill it in prior to the time you want to start writing your resume. You will certainly discover several strengths and may also discover areas for improvement. Most important, you will find several items sufficiently important to include on your resume – items that are keyed to recognized standards of effective teaching.

A TOUCH OF HUMOR

"One resume that came across my desk stated how the individual had won a contest for building toothpick bridges in middle school."

Qualifications	Self Rating
1. An engaging and enthusiastic personality	5 4 3 2 1
2. A passion for teaching	5 4 3 2 1
3. Establishes and maintains high behavioral expectations	5 4 3 2 1
4. Engages students in their lessons	5 4 3 2 1
5. Thorough knowledge of curriculum and standards	5 4 3 2 1
6. Plans that ensure academic achievement	5 4 3 2 1
7. Sets high academic expectations	5 4 3 2 1
8. Structures and delivers well-crafted lessons	5 4 3 2 1
9. Engages students in all lessons	5 4 3 2 1
10. Integrates technology into lessons systematically	5 4 3 2 1
11. Develops and maintains positive relationships with all students	5 4 3 2 1
12. Addresses the diverse needs of all students	5 4 3 2 1
13. Provides helpful and timely feedback	5 4 3 2 1
14. Engages students in critical thinking	5 4 3 2 1
15. Creates a strong classroom culture	5 4 3 2 1
16. Works in collaboration with other educators	5 4 3 2 1

My Teaching Philosophy

An activity I often share with students in one of my methods courses is to invite them to write out their personal philosophies of teaching early in the semester. That is, what do they believe and why do they believe those things are important in the academic success of children. My students have discovered that the writing of this philosophy can be one of the most powerful acts they do as pre-service teachers. It helps cement their beliefs and gives those beliefs some substance. The very act of writing down what you embrace can be both refreshing and instructive. True, a teacher's philosophy will change over time – mine certainly has over the course of the past four and a half decades. But, you won't know how much it changes until you take the time to record where you are...right now...philosophically.

This exercise also becomes quite valuable when students come to me asking for advice on how to begin drafting their resumes. I often suggest they write out their philosophy of teaching right in my office (no notes, no internet research, no re-reading of course textbooks). It's a painful process at first, but what students often come up with is a draft (a first draft, to be sure) of a document that can be invaluable as they start constructing their resumes. For, in no small measure, a philosophy is also a self-assessment – not only what you believe, but the strengths of those beliefs, too. By the way, they are encouraged to do additional drafts and bring them in to me for further review and critiquing.

Following is the Teaching Philosophy a former colleague of mine wrote several years ago as she was assembling her application packet for an elementary teaching position. It helped define her personal strengths and beliefs – and made the writing of her resume that much easier.

My Philosophy of Teaching

Lao-Tse once described an effective leader as one who imparts to his charges the feeling, "We did it ourselves!" So it is in the realm of teaching and learning.

An effective educator does not simply disseminate facts and figures, but acts as a catalyst, teaching (by example) a love for learning. By providing provocative questions rather than patent answers, children are led to discover knowledge; thus they become active participants in the learning process rather than passive receptors.

To be a successful "catalyst" requires a great deal. As a doctor selects the appropriate tool to execute a surgical procedure or an artist the correct brush to express a desired gesture, a teacher must have the knowledge and creativity to utilize a plethora of tools.

In order to meet the individual needs of students, an educator must skillfully incorporate visual, aural, and tactile activities via a variety of teaching strategies. However, even the wisest tactical decisions are rendered ineffective unless a climate of love, excitement, humor, and mutual respect is engendered.

To provide an environment that fosters both intellectual and emotional growth is a responsibility of the greatest magnitude. The reward, however, is of equal proportion if one is truly committed to leading children to love learning, life, and to say, "We did it ourselves!"

Not only was this document an important self-reflection, it also served as a template for my friend's professional resume. In short, she didn't have to craft her resume "out of thin air," rather she had crafted a statement of her beliefs that could be used in several places on the actual resume. Equally important, she had a statement that was perfect for the District's formal application – a statement that was inserted into the section entitled "What is your philosophy of teaching?" But the biggest bonus was that she had something that she could verbally share with an administrator during any interview. By planning this out well in advance of any interview, she had an impressive philosophy that any interviewer would be thrilled to hear.

✓EXTRA CREDIT:

You, too, will discover that one of the best self-assessments you can do is to construct a personal philosophy of teaching. Not only will this essay help you identify important attributes to include on a resume; so, too, will it become something you can use on an application form and, most certainly, something you can share as part of a job interview. The document, though short (approximately 300 words), can serve many purposes in your overall job search. It will take time to write, but it can pay big dividends in the end.

Here are some of the components you should consider as you prepare your own personal philosophy of teaching:

- **Your personality:** What are your personality traits, skills, talents, strengths, and experiences?

- **Your principles:** What are some of your character traits, beliefs, standards, expectations?

- **Your passion:** What "lights your fire," gets you excited, moves you, or inspires you when teaching?

- **Your vision:** What do you hope to be doing five or ten years from now? What professional goals have you set for yourself? What improvements would you like to make (in yourself or your teaching competence)?

- **Your impression:** What specific differences would you like to make in students' lives as the result of your teaching? What would you like students to say about you upon your retirement?

A TOUCH OF HUMOR

Included on one individual's resume:
"Personal Interests: Donating blood, fourteen gallons so far."

Chapter 5

<u>Shaping a Blockbuster Resume</u>

Let's start this chapter with some rules:

Rules for Interviews[1]:

- Maintain good eye contact.
- Always be prepared to ask questions of the interviewer.
- Always have a positive attitude.
- Demonstrate good listening skills.
- Exude passion for the position.

Rules for Food Preparation

- Always wash your hands before handling any food.
- Keep all kitchen surfaces meticulously clean.
- Cook food thoroughly.
- Avoid contact between raw foods and cooked foods.
- Always refrigerate perishable food.

Rules for Driving

- Always obey the posted speed limit.
- Buckle your seat belt.
- Give pedestrians the right of way when they're in a crosswalk.
- Always use your blinkers before making a turn.
- Never rev your Chevrolet Performance LT4 Supercharged 6.2L 650HP Engine when driving past a certain professor/author's house at 4:00 in the morning.

---

1   Fredericks, Anthony D. *Ace Your Teacher Interview: 149 Fantastic Answers to Tough Interview Questions* (Indianapolis, IN: Blue River Press, 2016).

Rules for Resumes

- There are no rules.

Yes, you read that right. There are lots of suggestions, tips, recommendations, advice, proposals, hints, expectations, ideas, and information…but no rules. Yes, there's some basic information that needs to be part of any well-written resume. But, beyond that you have some degree of discretion on how you will present that information and how you will use that information to highlight your skills and talents. The important thing to remember is that your resume needs to be 1) filled with high quality content, 2) aesthetically pleasing, 3) clearly written, and 4) error-free. Above all, it must exude professionalism. Indeed, one of the "tests" you can give yourself as you are writing your resume, is to ask yourself, "Would a professional add this (or do this) to her or his resume?"

Resume Ingredients

O.K., it's time for a confession. I cannot walk past a lemon meringue pie without breaking into an enormous smile, doing a little jig, or simply salivating on the spot. Lemon meringue pies (just writing that makes me drool) are my great weakness and I need considerable restraint in order to prevent myself from wolfing down an entire one in one fell swoop.[2] Truth be told, they are probably one of the greatest desserts ever created since the mass production of sugar or the discovery of the lemon tree in Assam (northeast India).

I mean, just look at the aesthetics. A puffy and lightly browned topping over a sinfully rich lemon-flavored and tart filling all baked inside a most delicious pastry shell. The array of complimentary colors (white, yellow, brown) are a visual delight. The aroma of a freshly baked pie sends all the senses into a wicked tailspin. And the perfect circular shape mirrors other beautiful circles in nature – sunflowers, a summer moon, and a jellyfish. Just the sight of a single lemon meringue pie tickles all my senses.

---

2 A good reason why my wife has to chaperone me whenever I go into a bakery.

And, then, there is the combination of ingredients that make a lemon meringue pie the quintessential dessert (a Google search revealed more than 400,000 different recipes for lemon meringue pie…WOW!). These ingredients are sufficient to tantalize any set of human taste buds:

Filling: sugar, flour, cornstarch, water, lemon juice, lemon zest, butter, egg yolks

Meringue: egg whites, sugar

It is the ingredients in your resume that will set it apart from all those other resumes sitting on a principal's desk and awaiting her or his review. Your resume's ingredients should be designed to help it stand out from the crowd; to help make it one of a kind. Your chosen ingredients determine how "delicious" your resume will be.

Here's the recipe:

A. Contact Data (expanded further in Chapter 6)

This is the information people need in order to contact you. Besides your name and address, it also includes phone numbers and e-mail addresses, along with other pertinent contact information (e.g. web site addresses). If a school district administrator wants to get hold of you quickly – say to invite you in for an interview – this is what she or he will need.

Sample:

Justin B. Burr

9275 Harmony Lane   justinb@xxx.com
Miami, FL 33131   www.webportfolio.com   (305) 555-1234

B. Objective (expanded further in Chapter 7)

What is the specific position you are applying for? It is critical that your objective is clearly matched with the specific job opening posted. If it is not, then a reader may be sufficiently confused to toss your application in the "NO" pile.

Sample:

Elementary School Teacher
2nd Grade

A TOUCH OF HUMOR

I have a feeling this particular applicant didn't get very many interviews. What do you think?

"Objective: My dream job would be as a professional baseball player, but since I can't do that, I'll settle on this."

C. Qualifications + Education/Certification (expanded further in Chapter 8)

The first part of this section sums you up in a few short, yet descriptive, sentences. It is both an autobiography and an advertisement. Most important, it is your first opportunity to truly sell YOU. For that reason, it will demand much of your time in its construction.

Sample:

Dedicated and devoted elementary teacher totally committed to the academic success of all students. Solid foundation in all curricular areas with special skills in dynamic reading strategies and intervention techniques for beginning readers. Talent as an educator focused on high-level cognition, problem-solving, and critical thinking opportunities across several subject areas. Embraces an inquiry-based philosophy of teaching – one that empowers students to take responsibility for their own learning.

The second part of this section lets the reader know that you are properly trained and properly certified. Here you will list your degree, your major and any minors, the institution from which you received (or will receive) your degree, and your G.P.A.

Sample:

Education

Bachelor of Arts, Elementary Education, Florida State University (Expected May 20__)

G.P.A. – 3.76/4.00

Certification

State of Florida, Elementary Education Certification, Grades K-6

INSIDER TIP

Write out the full name of your degree or expected degree (for example: Bachelor of Arts in Elementary Education). Also note that all degrees are written in the singular.

Include your G.P.A. if it is 3.0 or higher (for example: 3.76/4.00). If your G.P.A. is less than 3.0, do not include it.

Double check the exact title of the certification you will receive. Check with your college's Education Department or the Department of Education (Bureau of Teacher Certification) for your specific state.

D. Professional Teaching Experiences (expanded further in Chapter 9)

It is here that you will list, in reverse chronological order, the specific teaching experiences you have had throughout your college career. This includes student teaching and works backward through any field experiences or other teaching assignments related to the advertised position. This is where the "sell, don't tell" philosophy will clearly distinguish you from all the other candidates. It, too, will demand much of your time and effort.

Sample:

Professional Teaching Experience

Beachfront Elementary School – Clearwater, FL Spring 20__

Student Teacher (1st Grade)

- Designed and facilitated a theme-based first grade curriculum focused on self-awareness and self-concept.

- Developed a "Home and School" club for families that resulted in a 17% improvement in attitudes and a 97% participation rate by parents in homework assignments.

- Taught a first grade math unit on numeration that resulted in a 14% increase in scores on the Florida Standards Assessments (FSA).

- Developed an inquiry-based science unit (based on the book "Last Child in the Woods") with naturalists at the Cedar Key Natural Wildlife Refuge as part of the Summer Seashore Camp for primary-level students.

Horseshoe Crab Elementary School – Cedar Key, FL Fall 20__

Field Experience (2nd Grade)

- Integrated technology into the second grade social studies curriculum through the use of Nearpod, Prezis, virtual simulations, and Skype interviews with a local children's author.

- Engaged students in the learning process through an emphasis on multiple intelligences, differentiated instruction, and hands-on, minds-on teaching. District end-of-year tests showed an improvement of 13.8% over the previous year.

FROM THE PRINCIPAL'S DESK:

"Resumes should reflect your experiences with children, not always in a school setting, but focused on children. This shows the desire to want to work and interact with students, not just because the college requires observations and interactions."

E. Other Related Experiences (expanded further in Chapter 10)

This is the "value added" section of your resume – the part where you detail all the experiences you have had with young people specifically and with education in general. This is the section that completes your picture as a fully competent, dedicated and conscientious teacher. It establishes you as a well-rounded educator – one with many qualities to share with a school or district.

Included here may be some of the following categories: Special Skills, Public Speaking, Publications, Honors and Awards, Professional Affiliations, Community Activities, and Coaching Experiences.

Sample:

	Professional Profile
Affiliations	Florida State Reading Association Young Teachers Association
Honors and Awards	Outstanding Student Teacher – 20__ Dean's List – 20__ to Present
Public Speaking	Speaker, FSRT Conference, Orlando, 20__ Co-presenter, IRA Convention, Anaheim, CA (May 20__)
Languages	Fluent in English and Spanish
Special Skills	Volunteer volleyball coach – Seaweed Middle School Literacy tutor – Miami Literacy Council

FROM THE PRINCIPAL'S DESK:

"Don't be shy about listing your experiences with children, even if they are not formal teaching experiences. Knowing that a candidate is a scout leader or Sunday School teacher is relevant."

The Final Product

Included below is what a complete and well-designed teacher resume should look like. It is easy to read and allows a school administrator to obtain the essential information she or he needs in order to make a decision on whether to invite this applicant in for an interview. In a single page this individual has presented his strongest points, has effectively sold himself to any potential employer, and has focused on the needs of the reader moreso than on himself. This is a resume that will definitely get a second look!

Justin B. Burr

9275 Harmony Lane
Miami, FL 33131   www.webportfolio.com

justinb@xxx.com
(305) 555-1234

Elementary School Teacher

2nd Grade

Dedicated and devoted elementary teacher totally committed to the academic success of all students. Solid foundation in all curricular areas with special skills in dynamic reading strategies and intervention techniques for beginning readers. Talent as an educator focused on high-level cognition, problem-solving, and critical thinking opportunities across several subject areas. Embraces an inquiry-based philosophy of teaching – one that empowers students to take responsibility for their own learning.

Education

Bachelor of Arts, Elementary Education, Florida State University (Expected May 20__) G.P.A. – 3.76/4.00

Certification

State of Florida, Elementary Education Certification, Grades K-6

Professional Teaching Experience

Beachfront Elementary School – Clearwater, FL Spring 20__

Student Teacher (1st Grade)

- Designed and facilitated a theme-based first grade curriculum focused on self-awareness and self-concept.

- Developed a "Home and School" club for families that resulted in a 17% improvement in attitudes and a 97% participation rate by parents in homework assignments.

- Developed an inquiry-based science unit (based on the book "Last Child in the Woods") with naturalists at the Cedar Key Natural Wildlife Refuge as part of the Summer Seashore Camp for primary-level students.

Field Experience (2nd Grade)

- Integrated technology into the second grade social studies curriculum through the use of Nearpod, Prezis, virtual simulations, and Skype interviews with a local children's author.

- Engaged students in the learning process through an emphasis on multiple intelligences, differentiated instruction, and hands-on, minds-on teaching. District end-of-year tests showed an improvement of 13.8% over the previous year.

Professional Profile

Affiliations: Florida State Reading Association, Young Teachers Association

Honors and Awards: Outstanding Student Teacher Award – 20__, Dean's List – 20__ to Present

Public Speaking: Speaker, FSRT Conference, Orlando, 20__, Co-presenter, IRA Convention, Anaheim, CA (May 20__)

Languages: Fluent in English and Spanish

Special Skills: Volunteer volleyball coach – Seaweed School, Literacy tutor – Miami Area Literacy Council

INSIDER TIP

Notice there is not a heading for "References" or for "Hobbies." Do not list them on your résumé, nor should you include a statement that "References will be provided upon request." That's old school and will date you, showing that you've not taken the time to research current resume protocol.

A TOUCH OF HUMOR

Here's a candidate with a truly distinctive skill set: "Qualifications: I have extensive experience with foreign accents."

Chapter 6

<u>Framing Your Contact Data</u>

Several years ago I had a student who was truly exceptional! Jennifer (not her real name) was bright, enthusiastic, and absolutely committed to being a great classroom teacher. All her papers and classroom assignments were completed with zest, insight, and professionalism. It was very clear to me that she was going to be an outstanding teacher – one who would truly make a difference in the lives of students.

My opinions of her were confirmed during her student teaching semester when she got rave reviews from her college supervisor and excellent evaluations from her cooperating teacher. It was quite evident that she was making her mark, not only in the lives of the students she worked with, but also on colleagues and other professionals who saw a magnificent teacher in the making.

In the middle of her student teaching semester Jennifer began putting together her application packet including her cover letter, resume, (glowing) letters of recommendation, transcript, and a brief portfolio. She began sending out her packet to several schools with openings in New Jersey, Delaware, Maryland and Virginia. But, she heard nothing back from any of the 16 schools she had applied to. She was both frustrated and despondent.

She called me and scheduled a meeting to try and figure out why she wasn't being brought in for interviews in spite of a stellar record of achievement and very positive recommendations. I asked her to bring in her entire application packet so that she and I could review it together. When she arrived at my office she was clearly "down in the dumps." A big cloud was hanging over her head.

I picked up her resume and began to read it. Within a few seconds I knew why Jennifer – one of the best pre-service teachers I had ever had – was not being contacted for interviews. Here is the first part of her resume. See if you can discover why nobody was interviewing her (The answer is at the end of this chapter.).

Jennifer A. Thompson

6554 N. East St. (local)   564 Silverbell Lane (home)

York, PA 17405   Cherry Hill, NJ 08002

Objective: Third Grade Classroom Teacher

Qualifications:

When I pointed out her mistake*, Jennifer was devastated. Now, she understood why she wasn't getting any interview requests. But, I'm happy to report, there is a delightful ending to the story. Although she wasn't interviewed immediately after her student teaching semester, she did get a series of interviews about a month later (using her corrected resume). She is now teaching third grade in a dynamic and rapidly-growing school district in northern Virginia. Incidentally, she was voted "New Teacher of the Year" in her first year (She was in competition with 18 other new teachers hired that same year).

Here is what this book is all about: the primary objective of your resume is to get an interview. In order to do that you have to provide a certain amount of contact information so that any administrator reading your resume (and deciding, "Wow, this is a candidate we absolutely have to get in for an interview!") can get in touch with you quickly and easily. You want to make this process as straightforward and as simple as possible. If the administrator has to look up your contact information or has to do any other research in order to contact you, it is highly likely you will never be contacted, no matter how qualified you might be. It's essential you make yourself very easy to contact – you never know when someone might want to bring you in for an interview.

A TOUCH OF HUMOR

Here's what one candidate said on his resume:

"References: Please do not contact my immediate supervisor. My colleagues will give me a better reference."

Here are some suggested pieces of contact information you can list at the top of your resume so that potential employers can contact you easily. I'm not suggesting you include every one of these simply because a mass of data at the top of your resume might make it look cluttered and muddled (not a good first impression). Also, by placing too much information at the top of your resume you tend to take up valuable space (or lines) you want available for the remainder of your resume. You need to select the appropriate information with an eye on 1) ease of contact, 2) visual appeal, and 3) spacing considerations.

- ✓ Name
- ✓ Local street address
- ✓ Local city, state, zip code
- ✓ Home street address
- ✓ Home city, state, zip code
- ✓ Cell phone number
- ✓ Home phone number
- ✓ Campus phone number
- ✓ Personal email address
- ✓ Web page URL
- ✓ Online profile, such as LinkedIn
- ✓ Online resume or portfolio URL

Let's take a look at the four most critical pieces of contact information that should be at the top of every resume you write…no exceptions.

INSIDER TIP

If you have not done so already, be sure to create a LinkedIn profile. LinkedIn is a professional way of summarizing your accomplishments and presenting them to prospective employers. It also offers you the opportunity to include relevant experiences you don't have room for on a one-page resume – allowing people to learn more about you (should they choose to do so). However, instead of using the usual LinkedIn URL, be sure to create a custom URL to your public profile using instructions on the LinkedIn website. Then, make sure your custom URL is listed at the top of your resume. By the way, NEVER include your Facebook page on your resume – no matter how clean it is.

Name

Your name may be the most obvious item to include on your resume. That's true, but there are several factors you need to consider in order to do this correctly.

- In most cases you should list your full and complete name (the name on your driver's license or Social Security Card). You can, however, use an initial for a middle name. For example, you could list your name as William Andrews Bushnell or William A. Bushnell.

- If you have a nickname – a name you prefer to be called (instead of your formal name) then it is O.K. to list that as well. For example: Theodore ("Ted") A. Wilson.

- Be consistent. For example, if your formal name is Patricia Ellen McKay, but you list your name as Trish McKay (what all your friends call you), then there might be a misunderstanding between what you list on your resume and what is indicated on your official transcript of grades, for example. Play it safe – don't leave any doubt in a reader's mind that who you say you are is who you really are.

Make sure the font and size of your name on the resume and the font and size of your name on your cover letter are identical. This gives you a "personal brand" that makes you stand out from the crowd.

INSIDER TIP

If you have an unusual name, a name that might be difficult to pronounce, or a name that is gender-neutral, you can assist any readers by providing some additional information along with your name. Here are a few examples:

(Mrs.) Siani Andrews
Xiaofei (Sarah) Liu
Jan W. Burdett (Mr.)
(Mr.) Chris Webster
Sung-Wook "Sam" Baek
(Ms.) Michael Sampson
Nari Myeong (Myŏng)

Address

Another essential element of your contact information is your address. But, a word of caution is in order here. It would be to your advantage to list both your college address (and college contact information) along with your home address (and home contact information). If you are planning to graduate in the Spring semester and will then be moving home, you want prospective employers to be able to get hold of you in the most efficient way possible. If all you have on your resume is the college information, then it will become quickly outdated as soon as you move back home. A principal will be unable to get hold of you.

My advice, therefore, is to play it safe: list BOTH your college address AND your home address (or the address where you will be living after you graduate). Be sure to indicate which address is your current one and which address will be the one where you will be living when you leave the college. Take a look at the first part of the resume below and you will see how the candidate included this information.

Sample:

April Schauer

1234 Precipitation St. (prior to 5/14/20__)	9876 Torrential Rd. (after 5/14/20__)
Thundercloud, MT 59047	Flood, MS 38801
aprils@XXX.net	schauera@XXX.com
(406) 555-0000 (cell)	(228) 555-1111 (home)

Objective: High School Physical Education Teacher

Qualifications:

Telephone Number(s)

As much as 95% of the contacts made to potential teachers (for interview purposes) are done via phone. Making a phone call is quick, easy, and doesn't consume a lot of time for a very busy administrator. For most people reading this book, your cell phone number will be the one you want to list on every resume. Assuming you carry your cell phone with you wherever you may be, it will ensure that should a principal wish to invite you for an interview you will be easily accessible. That will allow you to reply instantly or, when you check for messages, to get back in a relatively short amount of time.

Depending on where you live or where you travel, you may find that cell coverage is spotty or inconsistent (say, you're going camping in the high desert of northern Arizona the weekend before final exams or deep sea fishing off Catalina Island at the end of the semester). In those cases, having your college or home phone number listed on your resume gives you extra assurance that a message can be left for you.

INSIDER TIP

Be sure to leave a professional voice-mail greeting on your cell phone. Messages such as, "Hey dude, you know what to do!" and "I'm either shopping or partying, but I'll be back sometime, so make it good." and "I'm probably totally smashed so I'll have to get back with you later, gator!" aren't going to do you any favors. Make sure your message is absolutely professional. If it isn't, then you can kiss the interview good-bye. Oh, a hip hop song, musical message, karaoke rendition, or personally authored poem won't work either. Best advice: Make sure your voice mail greeting is something your mother would approve!

"Extras"

Although optional, you may elect to include one or more of the following options as part of your contact information. Be careful, however, that the addition of these items doesn't muddle up the other information you've provided. If the resume appears to be too "top heavy" it may make it difficult for a reader to scan it and get the information needed in a short amount of time. When in doubt, always remember that "less is more."

- If you have your own personal web page you may elect to include this as part of your contact information. However, make sure that the information and graphics on your web page are education-related. Photos of your very cute pet iguana or the awesome time you had in Cancún over Spring Break won't do you any favors. If, on the other hand, your personal web page describes and highlights some of the educational experiences you've had throughout your teacher training program, then it may be appropriate to make that information available to any prospective employers.

- One of the best sites you can list on any resume is your LinkedIn profile. LinkedIn is a professional job search site that puts you and your qualifications out into the marketplace in a most professional manner. It is always to your advantage to include a LinkedIn profile as part of your application packet. Not only can it be updated frequently, but it also signals you as a professional educator.

If you have a teaching portfolio posted on any web site (you can easily create one on www.wix.com or www.weebly.com), then you may find it advantageous to list that as part of your contact information. In interview situations, many candidates have found it advantageous to have an electronic portfolio rather than dragging in a mountain of materials for a "show and tell" experience.

FROM THE PRINCIPAL'S DESK:

"Unfortunately, I have had the opportunity to come across contact information on documents that are not appropriate for school staff members. Emails that focus on sexual topics, binge drinking, etc. are a deterrent to getting an interview. Email addresses, blogs, Twitter accounts, Facebook accounts, etc. should have conservative names."

The Set Up

Following are examples of how you might want to set up your contact information:

Sample:

Ramona J. Wilkens
765 Timberline Drive, Frisco, CO 80443
(970) 555-1234 (C)
ramonaj@xxx.com

In this example, the candidate listed her entire address on one line. This helped save a line of text she could then use later in the resume. She also remembered to list her cell phone number as well as her personal email address.

Ramona J. Wilkens

765 Timberline Drive   (970) 555-1234 (C)
Frisco, CO 80443   ramonaj@xxx.com

This example highlights a "balanced" approach to resume design. In this case the applicant had an equal number of items to place on the left and right sides of the resume.

Ramona J. Wilkens

904 E. Ouray Ave. (prior to 5/15/20___)   765 Timberline Drive (after 5/15/20___)
Grand Junction, CO 81505   Frisco, CO 80443
970-555-1234 (cell)   970-555-9876 (home)
ramonaj@college.com   ramonaj@home.com

Here's another balanced approach that offers a lot of contact information and the specific dates when that information is valid. This set-up makes it very easy for an administrator to get hold of a potential candidate for an interview.

> # Ramona J. Wilkens
>
> 765 Timberline Drive
> Frisco, CO 80443 www.webportfolio.com
>
> ramonaj@xxx.com
> (970) 555-1234 (C)

In this example the candidate has created another example of balanced contact information. Except, in this case she has inserted a web site offering additional information for a reader.

> # Ramona J. Wilkens
>
> 765 Timberline Drive ramonaj@xxx.com C: (970) 555-1234
> Frisco, CO 80443 www.webportfolio.com H: (970) 555-9876

This example demonstrates a nice balanced approach with an abundance of contact information using very little space. Since only one address is listed, it is assumed that the applicant is a commuter student – she commutes to and from campus from her home.

* * *

Remember that your contact information may be the easiest to record, but that shouldn't lessen its importance. If someone can't get hold of you to schedule an interview, then all the work you put into the rest of the resume will go for naught. Start off on the right foot and you will be helping yourself (and the person reading the resume) immensely.

*The reason why Jennifer was not being contacted: She had neglected to include her cell phone number and her email address.

Chapter 7

<u>Write a Better Objective</u>

For a few years in high school I was on the basketball team. I loved the game – the opportunity to work together as a cohesive unit and master scripted plays made basketball more than just a pastime. It was also an opportunity to think strategically: to think about what a good outside shooter might do next or to think about how to quickly set up a zone defense to prevent a strong inside offensive game.

I loved practices – times when we could work on defensive and offensive plays designed to give us an advantage in certain game situations (or when I could perfect my fade-away jumper). But, there was a critical maxim a former coach always emphasized. It went something like this: "When all is said and done, there is only one strategy that will win the game for us: get it in the hoop… get it in the hoop!" Simple. Direct. To the point. Our coach had taken some of the most complex and complicated basketball principles and boiled them all down to a simple fact of life – the team that gets the ball in the hoop the most is the team that wins the game.

Later, as I began my teaching career, I kept hearing a corollary to my coach's statement: "K.I.S.S. – Keep It Simple, Stupid." In other words, the best solution to a problem or situation is often the simplest. When faced with obstacles, we frequently spend a lot of time looking for complex and complicated resolutions. We tend to overthink at times – ignoring the "forest for the trees" and mucking up a challenge with too much data. Just "get it in the hoop" my high school basketball coach would say; "Keep It Simple, Stupid" is what I now say (most often to myself).

That K.I.S.S. "philosophy" also works with resumes. Far too many applicants spend an inordinate amount of time crafting complicated and extravagant resumes designed to impress people; when, in fact, if they would just step back and simplify their document they could get their message across more efficiently and effectively. Nowhere is this truer than when you write the objective statement for your teaching resume.

INSIDER TIP

I'm going to let you in on a little secret - something that will put you heads and shoulders above 90% of the competition for any teaching position. That is, most applicants will use a "same old, same old" objective on every resume they send out. In short, one all-purpose objective will appear on every single resume they submit - whether those resumes are sent to urban schools, suburban schools, or rural schools; large schools or small schools; old schools or new schools, public schools or private schools. In essence, most applicants make a fatal and deadly mistake - they use the same dull objective over and over again.

Here's how you can rise above the competition and identify yourself as someone who is willing to "go the extra mile" to secure the teaching job of your dreams: Tailor your objective to the specific needs of the school or district advertising the position. That means you'll need to write a new, fresh, and original objective directed specifically to each and every targeted position. Will that be more work for you? Absolutely! But, you will be doing something that almost every one of your competitors will not. You will be identifying yourself as someone who is willing to do the extra work necessary to secure a specific position, rather than as someone who just follows the crowd.

The truth of the matter is that most teacher applicants (e.g. your competition for any posted position) will draft a single multi-function objective and insert it into every resume they send out. Here's a classic example of one of those all-purpose objectives:

OBJECTIVE: To discover a challenging position in an outstanding school district that will allow me to utilize my teaching skills and experiences in helping all children succeed in the classroom and throughout life.

Blah. Blah. Blah. Let me put it to you frankly – the objective above is filled with verbal garbage, rife with meaningless terms, and overflowing with boring and hackneyed vocabulary. It's an objective that could be used for every single teaching job ever posted in the Western Hemisphere since the beginning of recorded history. It's overweight, full of B.S., and flat out stinks! Even worse, it's all about the person who wrote it and has nothing to do with the position advertised by the school or district.

FROM THE PRINCIPAL'S DESK:

"Too many resume objectives are nothing more than hot air and empty words. After a while they all sound the same – boring."

Here are additional examples of puffy and meaningless objectives I've culled from a couple of teacher resumes:

OBJECTIVE: To make a significant difference in the lives of students and to advance my career as a dedicated and highly energetic teacher.

OBJECTIVE: To work as an elementary school teacher in a progressive district focused on academic achievement and community involvement.

OBJECTIVE: I would like to teach high school algebra and help students understand the role it plays in their everyday lives through rich and rewarding lesson plans.

OBJECTIVE: I am seeking a teaching job that will allow me to use my abilities, skills, and expertise to influence the next generation of students in becoming productive citizens and lifelong learners.

OBJECTIVE: To be a middle school teacher who will have a positive impact on youngsters during this trying time in their lives and to help them learn how social studies will be meaningful throughout their academic careers.

Here's a sad fact of life: objectives like the ones above have been used on resumes hundreds of thousands of times by past teacher candidates and will continue to be used hundreds of thousands of times by future teacher candidates. They've been read by hundreds of thousands of school principals and have been rejected by hundreds of thousands of school principals. They try to say everything; when, in fact, they say nothing.

A TOUCH OF HUMOR

I suppose the only thing this candidate left out of his objective was a silver BMW and a personal butler:

"OBJECTIVE: I need money because I have bills to pay and I would like to have a life, go out partying, please my young wife with gifts, and have a menu entrée consisting of more than soup."

Early in the book I shared an important number regarding the attention span of most resume readers: six seconds! In short, if you don't grab the attention of a reader within the first six seconds of reading a document as important as your job resume you will have given that person a very good reason not to read the remainder of your resume – no matter how good or how impressive it might be. Yet, the reality is that most teacher candidates will use bloated and meaningless objectives like those above. Any principal going through 200-300 applications for a single position and seeing statements similar to those above on most of those applications will automatically reject each and every one of them…simply because they all said the same thing – absolutely nothing! Bottom line: You want your resume to stand out, just as you want to stand out. If yours sounds like everyone else's, then it will probably wind up like everyone else's – in the trash can.

Take another look at the samples above and you will notice one consistent element in each one: All of them focus on what the applicant wants (e.g. "I am seeking a teaching job…."), rather than on what a specific school or district is advertising. So, here's another insider tip: If you write an objective about you, you will automatically doom your chances, just as 90% of the other applicants for the position will do. And, you'll help the reader make a very quick decision about the fate of your application: "Thanks, but no thanks!"

"So, what should I do?" you ask. Well, here are three critical keys to writing a good objective: 1) Your resume objective should echo a specific job posting. 2) Keep the emphasis off you and what you want. And, 3) K.I.S.S.!

Here are some examples:

> JOB POSTING: Immediate Opening – Fifth Grade Teacher
> **OBJECTIVE:** Fifth Grade Teacher
>
> JOB POSTING: Middle School Social Studies Teacher
> **OBJECTIVE:** Middle School Social Studies Teacher
>
> JOB POSTING: Classroom Teacher; Elementary School Classes;
> First Grade Teacher
> **OBJECTIVE:** First Grade Classroom Teacher
>
> JOB POSTING: Speech-Language Therapist/Pathologist
> **OBJECTIVE:** Speech Therapist
>
> JOB POSTING: High School Psychology Teacher
> (Grades 9-12)
> **OBJECTIVE:** Psychology Teacher (Grades 9-12)

A TOUCH OF HUMOR

I'd like to suggest that although this objective may be true for most of us, it's probably not a good idea to list it on a resume as this candidate did:

"OBJECTIVE: To hopefully associate with a millionaire one day."

In each of the samples above the objective is short, direct, and uses precise language from the specified job posting. Each objective is also focused on what the school or district wants, rather than on what the applicant desires. In short, a good objective is a targeted one, not a personal one.

Another advantage of a targeted objective is that is sends a very powerful message to the busy and overworked administrator reading it – "The applicant read my job posting and has tailored her or his resume specifically to my needs or wants."

FROM THE PRINCIPAL'S DESK:

"Most applicants never take the time or effort to customize their objective. They frequently use language developed by their college's career center. I wind up throwing about 80% of those resumes into the wastebasket."

In my conversations with school principals around the country they all told me they prefer a direct match between the actual job posting and an applicant's resume. A clearly defined objective that responds to the specific need(s) of a school or district will get considerably more attention than an objective that emphasizes what the applicant wants or needs. And, because your objective is specific to an identified job posting (without any of the bloated words that often accompany most objectives) it demonstrates that you and the advertised position are a well-matched pair. It's a guaranteed first step in nudging a very busy administrator to read more of your document.

It's that simple.

A TOUCH OF HUMOR

O.K., readers, try to top this one:

"OBJECTIVE: I would like to work for [an organization] that is very lax when it comes to tardiness."

(Dear Readers: I can't even make these things up!)

Chapter 8

Are You Qualified?

To open this chapter, let's consider a well-known professional football player – Peyton Manning. During the course of his 18-year playing career in the National Football League (NFL), Manning accomplished (among other records) the following:

- Won two Super Bowl Championships
- Named League Most Valuable Player (MVP) five times
- First quarterback in NFL history to win 200 games
- Selected to the NFL Pro Bowl 14 times
- Most career passing yards: 71,940
- Most passing yards in a season: 5,477
- Most career touchdown passes: 539
- Most touchdown passes in a season: 55

Now, let's take a look at the football career of the author of this book:

- High school football: 3 years (third-string right end)
- Passes caught: 1
- Yards run after catching pass: 2
- Touchdowns made: 0
- Number of varsity letters received: 0
- College scholarships offered: 0
- Number of cheerleaders dated after the "Big Game": 0

A quick glance (less than six seconds) at the records of these two football players and it is quite easy to determine which one is more deserving of being in The Pro Football Hall of Fame. In other words, it doesn't take long to assess the qualifications of these two individuals – one matches up quite well with the standards of the Hall of Fame; the other leaves… well, leaves much to be desired.

A TOUCH OF HUMOR

Here is an objective written by someone who obviously didn't proofread:

"Objective: Career on the Information Supper Highway."

INSIDER TIP

The "Qualifications" section is not a chronological overview of everything you've ever done in the field of education. Instead, it is a brief and focused presentation of personal data and philosophy that sells you as the ideal candidate for a specific position. In many cases, it may be one of the few items a busy administrator looks at as she or he reviews an enormous stack of applications for a posted position. It comes early in the sequence of sections on your resume; as a result it carries a great deal of weight and a great deal of importance. Consider it your professional "business card."

There are two different "Qualifications" you can effectively include in your resume: The "paragraph" format and the "paragraph + bullets" format. If you are just starting out and have limited teaching experiences, then the "paragraph" format would be an appropriate choice. On the other hand, if you have been in the profession for a while and have accumulated a diversity of experiences, then the "paragraph + bullets" format might be appropriate. Which one you select for your resume, however, is not critical; what is absolutely critical is that your Qualifications section, in a few select sentences, paints a complete picture of who you are and what you would bring to a specific position.

Here are two examples:

Paragraph Format

Qualifications

Dedicated and devoted elementary teacher totally committed to the academic success of all students. Solid foundation in all curricular areas with special skills in dynamic reading strategies and intervention techniques for beginning readers. Talent as an educator focused on high-level cognition, problem-solving, and critical thinking opportunities across several subject areas. Embraces an inquiry-based philosophy of teaching – one that empowers students to take responsibility for their own learning.

Paragraph + Bullets

Qualifications

Flexible, resourceful, and organized secondary social studies teacher who values active student engagement in history. Solid interpersonal skills that honor and respect students of all stripes in tandem with practiced classroom management strategies and all-inclusive lesson plans. Strong focus on teamwork and goal-setting strategies. Additional qualifications include:

• Differentiated classroom	• Authentic assessments	• Curriculum mapping
• Technology integration	• Character education	• Cross-curricular writing
• Critical thinking skills	• Cultural awareness	• Focus on literature

---

As you review the two samples above you will notice that they are not elaborate or extensive. However, in a very short space (and equally short amount of reading time), each of these two individuals has highlighted their skills, talents, and proclivities in a succinct and compact format. Any reader can quickly get a sense of each of these two individuals. Even more important, each of these two candidates has effectively created a *selling* document, rather than a *telling* one. The reader is now encouraged to read other sections of the resume, perhaps a little slower, but also with a keen awareness of someone who has clearly shown how she or he deserves further attention as a teacher candidate.

FROM THE PRINCIPAL'S DESK:

"Make sure the resume is specific to the district. General or all-purpose resumes seldom get noticed."

Education and Certification.

Any administrator reading your resume needs to know that you not only have the skills and talents for a position, but that you are also appropriately educated and certified. This is not an area you can wimp out on. You must be very clear and very precise in the data you include in this section. There should be absolutely no doubt in the reader's mind that you have (or will soon have) the necessary authorization(s) from the appropriate credentialing agency(ies). If you do not note your certification on your resume, it is highly likely that an administrator will assume that you don't have it (or are not expecting it in the near future) and your application materials will quickly find their way into someone's trash can.

You have several choices on how you can profile your education and certification. There is no single preferred format. Select the one you are most comfortable with from the examples below:

Format #1

Education

Master of Education, Reading, Florida State University
(Expected Spring 20___)

Bachelor of Arts, Education, Florida State University, 20___

Certification

State of Florida, Middle School Certification, Grades 5-8

Format #2

Teaching Certifications & Education

- Certified Secondary Teacher (English, Grades 7-12), Commonwealth of Pennsylvania, 20__

- Certified Reading Specialist (grades K-12), Commonwealth of Pennsylvania, 20__

- Master of Education Candidate, Very Big State University, expected 20__

- Bachelor of Science, Elementary Education, Costmore University, 20__

Format #3

Education

Doctor of Education Degree	University of California, Irvine (Expected 20__)
Master of Education Degree	University of California, Los Angeles (20__)
Bachelor of Education Degree	University of Nevada, Las Vegas (20__)

Certifications

Preliminary Multiple Subject Credential	California
General Provisional Teacher of Young Children	Nevada

It's a Match!

You'll remember from the previous chapter that it is very important for you to write your objective using the exact words of the job posting. We discussed several reasons why this is significant. Here's another one: by stating a very precise objective you can assist the reader in quickly determining whether your certification is a direct match for that objective. This is one of the things a reader needs to do during that six second perusal of your resume. If you write a long-winded and "fluffy" objective you will make the reader work too hard to determine a match. The result will often be that the resume gets rejected simply because it wasn't abundantly clear that the objective and the certification were in agreement.

FROM THE PRINCIPAL'S DESK:

"We look for someone who can follow directions. If you can't follow directions on the application process, how will you teach your students to follow directions in the classroom?"

It's "Quiz Time" again! In the chart below match an item in the first column to its corresponding item in the second column. In other words, you are going to match a stated objective (on the resume) with its most appropriate certification (Note: Answers are at the bottom of the page.[1])

Stated Objective	Certification
High School Biology Teacher	Middle School (Grades 5-8) – Math
Grade 7 Math Teacher	Special Education – Education of Deaf
Fourth Grade Classroom Teacher	Class 2 Educator License – Elementary Education
Teacher of Deaf Students	Preliminary Teaching License – Secondary Education, Biology

That was relatively easy, wasn't it? Great! Now, let's do another matching activity. For this one I'm going to list some "fluffy" objectives that were obtained from resume writers who didn't read this book (especially Chapter 7). Then, in the second column I'm going to list the stated teaching certificates required of those applicants (and listed) as part of several on-line recruitment notices. See if you can match them up.

Stated Objective	Certification
To work as a dynamic teacher in a progressive district focused on academic achievement and community involvement.	Elementary Education – PreK – 4

---

1 1 - D , 2 - A , 3 - C , 4 - B

I am seeking a teaching job that will allow me to use my abilities, skills, and expertise to influence the next generation of students in becoming productive citizens and lifelong learners.	Interdisciplinary Early Childhood Education (Birth to Primary)
To discover a challenging position in an outstanding school district that will allow me to utilize my teaching skills and experiences in helping all children succeed in the classroom and throughout life.	Teacher of Students with Disabilities (7-12)
To make a difference in the lives of students and to advance my career as a dedicated and highly energetic teacher.	Middle Grades Science Teacher (grades 5-9)

Pretty confusing? Right! [NOTE: I'm not able to provide answers to the second quiz simply because I can't even figure them out!].

What I'm sure you've noticed by now is that a reader of your resume has to get certain (very important) information in a short amount of time. Therefore, it's critical to the success of your resume that there is a very close match between the position you're applying for (Your stated objective) and the education/certification profiled on your resume. If that match is not easily apparent, then it is highly likely a reader will move on to someone else's resume.

A TOUCH OF HUMOR

Here's an interesting talent listed by one candidate: "Skills: Being bi-lingual in three languages."

Chapter 9

Shine the Light on Your Experiences

Let's begin this chapter with another quiz...a fairly easy quiz. Take a look at the two boxes below. In Box A are two statements. Box B also has two statements. Read the statements in both boxes and then answer the question that follows. Ready? Go.

> **A.**
>
> Launched an after-school science club for fourth grade students that resulted in a 23% improvement on the PSSA exams.
>
> Researched and designed a multimedia social studies unit on the impact of the railroad on changing social standards in the late 1800s – a unit now incorporated into the 11th grade curriculum at Excellent Area High School.

> **B.**
>
> My duties included passing out homework assignments, taking attendance, and monitoring all quizzes and exams.
>
> I was responsible for setting up the gymnasium before students arrived as well as cataloging all the equipment and supplies.

Which statements did you find to be most compelling and/or most interesting?

❏ Those in Box A

❏ Those in Box B

Professional Teaching Experiences

Like most people, you probably found the statements in Box A to be the most descriptive and the most interesting. Those statements, or professional teaching experiences, were full of action and indicated specific results. Why? It all had to do with the verbs used in each of the statements. Verbs such as "launched," "researched," and "designed" enhance each statement with clear and convincing language. On the other hand, commonly used resume phrases such as "My duties included…." and "responsible for…." are passive in nature. They say so little and are so frequently used on hundreds of thousands of resumes each year that they have absolutely no impact. There is nothing about those phrases that distinguishes or clearly differentiates a candidate (like you) from every other candidate also applying for the same position.

INSIDER TIP

Here's a list of commonly used (and over-used) phrases (HINT: These are phrases you want to eliminate from your resume):

- "Duties included…."
- "Responsible for…."
- "Responsibilities included…."
- "Able to organize…."
- "Am passionate…."
- "Am creative…."
- "Am motivated…."
- "Can organize…."
- "Can problem-solve…."
- "Have extensive experience…."
- "Am driven…."

Use any of the phrases listed above in your resume and you will be identifying yourself as one of the crowd, rather than as one of a kind.

The overwhelming problem with all the phrases in the box above is that, for the most part, they show up on far too many resumes. And, they are far too general – offering little in the way of specific details about who you are and what you have done. I hate to be blunt, but you and about a million other candidates were responsible for many things during your student teaching experience (that makes you one of a crowd). On the other hand, if you write, "Instructed three first grade ELL students resulting in sight word gains of from 24% – 37% over a four-week period" then you have clearly and convincingly differentiated yourself from everyone else (and that makes you one of a kind).

The Most Powerful Words in the World

The key, ultimately, is in the verbs you use for each of the bullet points on your resume.

INSIDER TIP

- Begin each bullet point (in your "Experiences" section) with an "action verb" – usually in the past tense.
- The verbs you choose should clearly define what you did and the results you achieved.
- Eliminate the word "I."

Beginning each bulleted accomplishment statement with a strong action verb helps to highlight your successes and allows a reader to get a sense of your skills by quickly scanning the page (in six seconds) prior to reading each individual bullet point. Always vary the action verbs on your resume in order to demonstrate a wide assortment of talents. Here is a list of verbs to help you get started.

A
Achieved
Acted
Adapted
Adjusted
Administered
Advanced
Advised
Altered
Analyzed
Answered
Arranged
Assembled
Assessed
Assisted
Augmented

B
Balanced
Briefed
Built

C
Calculated
Categorized
Certified
Chaired
Charted
Classified
Coached
Collaborated
Collected
Combined
Communicated
Compiled
Composed
Computed
Conducted
Constructed

Consulted
Controlled
Converted
Coordinated
Counseled
Created

D
Decided
Decreased
Defined
Delegated
Delivered
Demonstrated
Designed
Determined
Developed
Decided
Diagnosed
Differentiated
Directed
Distributed
Documented
Drafted

E
Edited
Educated
Eliminated
Empowered
Enabled
Encouraged
Enhanced
Enlarged
Ensured
Established
Estimated
Evaluated
Examined

Executed
Expanded
Expedited

F
Facilitated
Filed
Formulated
Fostered
Fulfilled Gained
Gathered
Generated
Grew
Grouped
Guided

H
Handled
Headed

I
Identified
Illustrated
Implemented
Improved
Increased
Influenced
Informed
Initiated
Innovated
Inspected
Installed
Instituted
Instructed
Integrated
Interviewed
Invented
Investigated

L

Launched
Lectured
Led
Logged

M

Maintained
Managed
Measured
Mentored
Monitored
Motivated

N

Negotiated

O

Obtained
Operated
Orchestrated
Ordered
Organized
Originated
Oversaw

P

Performed
Persuaded
Planned
Posted
Prepared
Presented
Processed
Produced
Proposed
Provided

R

Realized
Recommended
Recorded
Redesigned
Referred
Reorganized
Repaired
Reported
Represented
Researched
Resolved
Responded
Restructured
Revamped
Reviewed
Revised
Revitalized

S

Scheduled
Selected
Separated
Served
Serviced
Set goals
Set up
Simplified
Solved
Specified
Started
Stimulated
Strategized
Streamlined
Strengthened
Studied
Summarized

Supervised
Supported

T

Tested
Tracked
Trained
Transformed
Translated
Troubleshot

U

Updated
Upgraded

V

Verified

W

Weighed
Won

A TOUCH OF HUMOR

Maybe it's me, but I'm not quite sure what this candidate was applying for:

"I have had experience in logic programming, basic software creation, bear wrestling, and am fluent in C++."

An Inside Secret

I recently read a story about a professional teacher recruiter who attended a teacher recruitment fair in a large metropolitan area. During the course of her day she received hundreds of resumes from eager applicants – all of whom were just finishing up their student teaching semester and all of whom were eager to obtain a full-time teaching position. In reading those resumes, she lamented the fact that more than 80% of the students described their student teaching experiences with the following three bullet points:

- Assisted cooperating teacher
- Developed lesson plans
- Managed student discipline issues

What she found most distressing was that none of those students took the time or made the effort to *differentiate* their experiences and accomplishments. In short, they all used the same phrases and they all followed a similar template. As a result (and I know this is going to sound cruel and harsh), she wound up tossing all those resumes in the trash before she left the building.

Take a look again at the three bulleted statements in the paragraph above. Guess what – every student teacher since the beginning of recorded history has done those three tasks. I've done them, my colleagues have done them, the thousands of undergraduate students I have taught in my college's teacher education program has done them, and every teacher in every school in every state, province, and territory throughout the entire Western Hemisphere has done them. In short, we've all had three identical experiences.

Here's the key: Separate yourself from the crowd. Make your accomplishments clearly different and distinctive from everyone else's. Make yourself stand out as a unique and highly qualified prospective teacher – one who has accomplished some great things and achieved some great results.

FROM THE PRINCIPAL'S DESK:

"Make sure you include lots of field experiences, practicums, and other life experiences related to education or work with kids."

Look at these examples:

- Designed and facilitated a theme-based kindergarten curriculum focused on self-awareness and self-concept.

- Re-organized and catalogued all Physics Lab equipment. Received letter of appreciation from Dr. Woody Forrest, principal of Timber High School.

- Developed a "Home and School" club for families that resulted in a 17% improvement in attitudes and a 97% participation rate by parents in homework assignments.

- Authored an inquiry-based science unit (based on the book "*Last Child in the Woods*") with naturalists at Crystal River County Park for all third-grade students in Garfield County.

- Presented a workshop ("*Into the Night: New York and the Underground Railroad*") at the Northeastern History Educator's Association's annual conference.

- Planned and executed **Everyday Math Program** for fifth grade students at Skip Roper Elementary School resulting in a 22% improvement in PSSA scores.

INSIDER TIP

Write all your numbers in their numerical form, rather than in their written form ("22%" rather than "twenty-two percent"). When numbers are written numerically they pop out, catch the eye of the reader, and get more emphasis. They also take up less space – space you might need for other information in your resume.

- Trained and experienced in integrating multiple intelligences in a variety of children's literature. Demonstrated M.I. procedures to all 4th grade teachers at Maniacal Elementary School.

- Consulted with special-education teachers and guidance counselors in the development of a unique model of geometry instruction for five special-education inclusion students.

- Coordinated and implemented IEPs for developmentally disabled students. Administered Woodcock-Johnson assessments for initial and re-evaluation referrals.

- Planned and executed a weekly storytelling program at Martin Memorial Library for pre-school youngsters and their parents. The program was directly responsible for a 36% increase in books checked out of the Children's Section over the course of the ten week project.

FROM THE PRINCIPAL'S DESK:

"Include experiences more than just those you did in student teaching. Did you work at a summer camp or other job that involved kids? I want to know."

One thing should be clear from your review of the accomplishments listed above. They are all unique. They are all singular. They are all distinctive. Unlike "Developed lesson plans," the statements above are specific to a particular individual. They separate that individual from the rest of the crowd. Most important, they relate a unique story of initiative, accomplishment, achievement, and potential. In other words, you'll stand out as a teacher any administrator would be delighted to interview.

You can really help yourself by remembering the "six-second" rule. Or, ask yourself this question: Which words on your resume can you guarantee a principal or personnel manager will read when they're skimming hundreds of teacher resumes? Aside from your name and degree, it's going to be the very beginning of each bullet. So get their attention by using strong, powerful, specific verbs that make you stand out.

Here are some examples:

This description...	stands out better than...
• Developed and implemented a Nearpod lesson focused on....	• I was assigned to write some lesson plans on the Civil War....
• Organized an outdoor education unit on riparian invertebrates that resulted in....	• I took students to the local park and worked with them....
• Designed a 2nd grade family blog that increased parent involvement by....	• My cooperating teacher and I put together an outreach program for parents....
• Launched an after-school writing project for 11th grade students that produced....	• I helped some students improve their writing skills by staying after school and....
• Redesigned 8th grade trigonometry lessons on cosine, sine, and tangent; students demonstrated an overall improvement of....	• The trigonometry lessons on cosine, sine, and tangent were too difficult, so I wrote some new....

Here's a tip that will clearly differentiate your resume from most of the others submitted for a classroom position. Most candidates submit resumes that simply tell a reader what their duties were – specifically during their student teaching experience (a good example of "same old, same old."). For the most part those duties are familiar, similar, and predictable. On the other hand, a resume that stands out...one that is clearly different from all the others... is one that focuses, not on duties, but rather on accomplishments. In other words, it's not about what you were responsible for, but rather about what you made happen.

Here's the bottom line: A resume should be all about accomplishments (active), not duties (passive).

Let's Put It All Together

Now, let's begin to put together some powerful and distinctive accomplishment statements. These statements should be listed under each position you have included on your resume ("Student Teaching," for example). Each statement should be bulleted and each statement should reference all of the following elements: what you did in the position, how you did it, and the results of your actions.

> ## A TOUCH OF HUMOR
>
> I wish I had thought of listing this one on my resume: "Hobbies: Having a good time."

In order to help you generate a perfect set of Professional Teaching Experience statements for your resume I'd like to offer the following easy-to-use formula:

Bullet Point with Action Verb + Statement + Example + Result

1. Bullet Point with Action Verb: Select a powerful verb from the lists above. Since you will be crafting several accomplishment statements it is suggested that you use a variety of verbs with those statements to demonstrate your unique skills and diversity of talents.

Bullet Point with Action Verb:

- Designed

2. <u>Statement</u>: Write an accomplishment statement beginning with your chosen action verb. Do not begin any accomplishment statement with a personal pronoun ("I," for example).

Bullet Point with Action Verb and Statement:

- Designed a fourth grade science unit.

3. <u>Extension</u>: Expand your statement (above) by providing some specifics or examples as to what you actually did.

Bullet Point with Action Verb, Statement and Example:

- Designed a fourth grade science unit on physical and chemical changes in matter.

4. <u>Result</u>: State what was achieved as a result of your action(s). In other words, what was the purpose of doing what you did?

Accomplishment Statement with Bullet Point, Action Verb, Statement, Example, and Result:

- Designed a fourth grade science unit on physical and chemical changes in matter that resulted in a 14% increase in scores on the annual PSSA exams.

See how easy it is? I hope you can also see that these accomplishment statements are much more powerful and much more eye-catching than something like "I was responsible for teaching fourth grade science during the last four weeks of student teaching." Well-constructed accomplishment statements get a principal to notice you: they are the kinds of statements that separate you from the crowd and make you unique, the kind of statements that encourage a reader to want to bring you in for an interview.

INSIDER TIP

Never include more than 6-7 bullet points for any specific position (even if your only listed position is "Student Teaching"). Keep the "six second" rule in mind. No matter how impressive your bullet points are, a busy administrator isn't going to have the time or inclination to read an expansive list of bullet points. Cut, reduce, or condense where necessary.

Please remember that your experiences are critical determinants of a successful resume. Using powerful verbs in conjunction with verifiable results can easily set you apart – in a very positive way – from all the other candidates. This is particularly important for positions that get lots of applicants. If a busy administrator only devotes about six seconds to each resume, you want to be sure she or he picks up the most important and essential elements of your resume as her or his eyes sweep across your document. You can help them out (as well as yourself) when you focus on a few key elements designed to capture their attention.

FROM THE PRINCIPAL'S DESK:

"I want something I can look at fast. I need to get the information quickly."

Chapter 10

Other Related Essentials

✓EXTRA CREDIT:

I'd like to invite you to participate in three (strange) activities:

Drive to a donut shop (Dunkin' Donuts, for example) in your town. As you walk in the door focus your eyes on the display racks with all the donuts in full view of patrons. Don't look at any of the signs or labels indicating the various flavors - just look at all the donuts on display. After about six seconds, turn your back and quickly write down brief descriptions of those donuts that captured your attention (i.e. chocolate with sprinkles, vanilla and caramel stripes, etc.).

After your donut shop experience drive to a new car dealership in town. Walk in the showroom and quickly look around. What do you notice in a six-second visual sweep of the room?

After getting an eyeful of new cars, it's time to drive on over to the nearest cell phone store. Take a quick look at some of the latest models. What makes them stand out? What makes some models more attractive than other models? What features do you want on your next cell phone that you currently don't have?

What was similar about all three activities? For a large portion of the time you were in each of those stores you tended to focus on the "extras." Like many people (especially this author) you were attracted to all the sprinkles, nuts, crunchies, and other treats that often adorn the tops of several different varieties of donuts. In the car dealership you may have focused on the variety of colors, the rims of the wheels, the design of the mirrors or front grill moreso than on the basics of the car (engine, tires, steering wheel, etc.). When you were in the phone store you, most likely, looked at several of the added features of new phones that would help you stay more connected with your friends and associates. It was less about the basic phone and more about the special touches that made a model clearly stand out from its competition.

In all three cases you attention was, in many cases, drawn not to the basics of a donut, car, or cell phone – but rather to some of the extra features, special additions, or unique characteristics. It was those "extras" that caught your attention and, perhaps, even enticed you to look closer at a product than you might have otherwise (Put some multi-colored sprinkles on a chocolate-covered donut and it has my immediate attention every time.).

You can add "sprinkles" to your resume, too. These are items that will clearly distinguish you from other candidates – items that will make you stand out and get noticed. These are the additional qualifications you add to your resume to demonstrate your overall value to a principal and why that principal should bring you in for an interview.

Related Experiences

The remainder of this chapter catalogs several different kinds of Related Experiences you may want to include on your resume. It is important to remember that these are not "fillers" – items listed just to "pad" your resume or extend it to a full page. These are items that highlight your versatility, your range of professional experiences, and your desire to make a sincere difference in the lives of children. Don't make the mistake, however, of including as many of these as you possibly can. Some may be appropriate depending on your experiences and others will be inappropriate. For example, if you don't have any professional publications don't include PUBLICATIONS on your resume just so you can list that wonderful essay you wrote about your very talented dog when you were in sixth grade. By the same token, if you don't have any education-related HONORS AND AWARDS, please don't list the third place ribbon you won for Sheep Showmanship at the local farm show ten years ago just to include this category. As a general rule of thumb, only include items or events from your Freshman year in college forward. High school, middle school, and elementary school achievements are, for the most part, inappropriate.

Each of the following categories is optional. You may wish to include one or more depending on your specific set of experiences. Review this list and determine if specific categories are pertinent to you. If they are, include them; if they aren't, forget them. As you review these categories also consider including summer, part-time and volunteer positions for inclusion in this section. Principals are interested in hiring well-rounded individuals who bring a wealth of teaching-related talents, skills and experiences to their schools. If you worked as a camp counselor, a teacher aide, or a Sunday School teacher (all education-related), then you should make those experiences visible to any reader of your resume.

FROM THE PRINCIPAL'S DESK:
"What have you done beyond student teaching?"

Special Skills

It is quite likely you have one or more special skills or talents that could be highlighted on your resume. These skills can give your qualifications for a specific position added value and clearly distinguish you from other candidates applying for the same position. For example, you may have talents in any of the following areas: foreign languages, technology skills, tutoring English Language Learners, bullying prevention, or musical productions. As you should with all other entries in this part of your resume, make sure anything you list here has an educational connection – specifically, a connection with the job to which you are applying. For example, the position may be for a middle school English teacher; however, listing a special skill such as Assistant Mechanic – Bob's Auto Repair won't do you any favors (Hint: leave it out). On the other hand if you have worked as a tutor at your college's Writing Center for two years, then that would be appropriate to include. If the school you are applying to is in an area with a significant Latino population and you happen to be bilingual in both English and Spanish, then that is a skill that needs to be featured here. Other examples include:

Special Skills

- Fluent in four languages: English, Spanish, Farsi, Portuguese
- Competent in the following computer platforms and tools: Adobe, BlazeDS, Eclipse/Flex Builder, Flash, Illustrator, MySQL, Photoshop, SQLite, Tomcat
- Mathematics tutor - Wildebeast University Math Clinic (20__ to Present)
- Assistant J.V. Coach, Football - High Desert High School, Arid, CA (20__ to 20__)

FROM THE PRINCIPAL'S DESK:

"One candidate listed as a quality - professional clown. Unfortunately, the candidate did not get employed by the district, but we certainly noticed him in the pile of applicants."

Public Speaking

Undergraduate students are often provided opportunities to attend local, regional, and national conferences, symposiums, colloquia, conventions, and other education meetings. These are wonderful opportunities to share your expertise in a particular topic, in addition to getting some inside information from leaders in your field. They offer an opportunity to "rub elbows" with experts and practitioners allowing you to expand your educational experiences.

If you have been invited to present at an educational meeting, make sure that experience is included as a vital part of your resume. Here are some examples:

Presentations

- Poster Presentation: "Tombstone: The Forgotten Story." Arizona History Symposium, Prescott, AZ, April 20__.

- Co-presenter (with Dr. Brooke Trout and Dr. Sal A. Mander): "Diversity of Riparian Life in and Around the Streams of Custer National Forest," South-Central Montana Ecological Association, Billings, MT, May 20__.

- Speaker, "Integrating Nearpod into the Secondary Social Studies Curriculum," March 20__, National Social Studies Conference, Washington, DC.

Publications

One of the ways you can clearly distinguish yourself from the competition is with a list of various types of publications. Publications demonstrate your commitment to the profession and your desire to help other becomes successful educators. If you have been teaching for some time and have submitted articles to various professional publications, the addition of a PUBLICATIONS section to your resume can carry a lot of weight. By the same token, if you are an undergraduate and have worked with a professor on a co-authored project, that should be noted as well.

This section will not be applicable to everyone. However, if you have done any of the following then they should be included in a special section: blog, instructional manual, articles, online web site content, course manuals, curriculum guides, pamphlets, or teacher guides. Here are some examples:

Publications

- Co-author with Dr. Barbara Seville, "Literacy Education Challenges and the Common Core," *Southeast Educator's Journal*, Vol. 34, pp. 65-68, 20___.

- "Strategies in Phonemic Awareness," New Hampshire Elementary Educators, May 20___, pp. 15-17.

- First Grade Teacher's Guide - "Activities for Beginning Readers" - Long River School District, Long River, IL (20___)

Honors and Awards

If you have been awarded significant awards or citations during your college years, it would be most appropriate to create a separate section for them at the bottom of your resume. This section provides an interesting piece of "visual dessert" near the bottom of your document. Here's how you might want to record those awards:

Honors and Awards

- Phi Delta Kappa Student Teacher of the Year Award, Spring 20___.

- Recipient, "Making a Difference Award" from the Alpha Beta College Department of Education.

- Magna Cum Laude Graduate, Not Yale University, Spring 20___.

- Dean's List - seven consecutive semesters - Demanding College

A TOUCH OF HUMOR

Apparently, someone (at least on his resume) thought all the following should be listed:

"Skills: creativity, bravery, arrogance, cleverness and honesty."

Professional Affiliations

If you belong to professional education groups it would be appropriate to list those in your resume. Those groups may be local, regional, or national organizations; however, it is very important that any you list are education affiliated. Playing the trumpet in a local jazz group or serving as vice-president of a student political action committee are not activities you want to list on your resume. True, they do underscore a diversity of interests and pastimes, but they do not enhance your educational qualifications for a specific teaching position. They should be excluded. Here are some examples of what to include:

Professional Affiliations

- College Representative, Deep Valley Mathematics Teachers Association, 20__ to Present.
- Vice-President, Sigma Sigma Sigma Chemistry Association - Charleston Area Group, 20__ to 20__.
- Volunteer, Flatiron Wildlife Refuge Education Committee, 20__ to Present.

Community Activities

Many principals want to know if you have engaged in activities or endeavors that go beyond the usual requirements of any college's education department. For example, all students participate in student teaching experiences during their teacher training program. However, if you also volunteered to lead a teen book discussion group at the local public library or worked with your local literacy council to help ELL students learn to speak and write English, then those would be valuable assets to profile on your resume. They would also identify you as someone willing to do something extra...to go above and beyond... certainly an attribute any principal would embrace. Following are some examples:

Community Activities

- Assistant Den Leader, Cub Scout Pack #1234, Newport Beach, CA, 20__ to 20__.
- Volunteer, Eagle Claw Middle School "Science is for Girls Club," 20__ to 20__.
- Tutor, Lazy Mountain Municipal Library Homework Project, Lazy Mountain, UT, 20__ to 20__.

Coaching Experience

If you have done any kind of coaching or have worked with athletics in any capacity, then it would be valuable to list those experiences in this section. While this might be particularly important for positions at the middle school and secondary levels, it could also be critical for elementary positions as well. It is not unusual for elementary teachers to serve as coaches or assistant coaches on high school or middle school teams (One of my former colleagues, an exceptional Kindergarten teacher, also served as the varsity wrestling coach at the local high school.)

Coaching Experience

- Assistant Coach, Lake Superior Little League (Winkler's Red Sox), Duluth, MN, Summer 20__ to Summer 20__.
- Weights Trainer - JV football team, Jim Shorts Regional High School, Faraway, TX (Fall 20__ to Fall 20__).
- Tennis coach, Camp Lotsa Mosquitoes, Assateague, VA, 20__.

Pulling It All Together

In including these extra qualifications in your resume you may encounter a challenge. That is, how can I present all my extra skills without using up a lot of space? As you might imagine, it would be most inappropriate to have a resume of three or four pages just so you have sufficient space to include all the extras. On the other hand, if you just have a few items, setting up a series of "boxes" as in the illustrations above, would create a visual nightmare for any potential reader (a hodgepodge of information spread over a large visual field).

INSIDER TIP

Scan your resume for any acronyms. Write out the full name of the title, organization, name, or certification and the acronym the first time they are listed. This will help a reader know exactly what you are talking about. For example: Multiple Intelligences (M.I.), Individualized Education Plan (IEP), Least Restrictive Environment (LRE), Parent Advisory Committee (PAC), and Special Education (SPED). After the first time the full name and acronym are used, it is then acceptable to use just the acronym.

A TOUCH OF HUMOR

Here's a candidate who, if nothing else, truly helped the reader make a quick decision:

"Here are my qualifications for you to overlook."

This is when you might want to consider a single box – one that groups all your special skills into a neat, compact, and easily "digestible" area. Besides consolidating a lot of varied information in a single unit, this arrangement presents that data in a professional and very readable format.

Take a look at this example:

Professional Teaching Experiences

Affiliations   Arizona State Reading Association
Maricopa County Literacy Council (Vice President)
Young Teachers Association - Phoenix Chapter

Honors and Awards   Outstanding Student Teacher Award - 20__
Dean's List - 20__ to Present

Public Speaking	Speaker, ASRT Conference, Tucson, 20__
	Co-presenter, IRA Convention, Anaheim, CA (May 20__)
Languages	Fluent in English and German
Special Skills	Volunteer track coach (distances) - Saguaro High School
	Literacy tutor - Phoenix Area Literacy Council

It is highly unlikely you would include all of the categories above on your resume. However, carefully consider the addition of two or three of those categories as essential elements of your overall resume. In doing so, you will set yourself apart from the competition. You will be demonstrating to a principal that you have gone "above and beyond" and, in so doing, you have demonstrated your potential for any school or district. The "extras" showcase your added value to a school and help you stand apart from the crowd. Not surprisingly, it is often the "extras" that can propel you to an interview.

FROM THE PRINCIPAL'S DESK:

"I want to know about all the extra-curricular experiences you've had that are connected to education."

Chapter 11

<u>The Visual Impression</u>

Back in Chapter 2, I talked about the "Six Second Rule" the research data which demonstrated that most resume readers spend only about six seconds reading a resume. Simply because school administrators have often seen thousands or tens of thousands of resumes over their professional career, they know what to look for in any new resume. In six seconds they can determine if a particular applicant has included pertinent, necessary and relevant information on their resume. In those six seconds they look for specific patterns, essential bullet points, critical clusters of information, and key words. Having read so many resumes they know exactly what should be on an outstanding resume and whether necessary information is missing or is entirely out of order.

Now, that said, let's create a scenario. Imagine you have been invited to a weekend party at an off-campus location. Let's say it's in celebration of a familiar holiday (Halloween, St. Patrick's Day, Cinco de Mayo, etc.). Most important, you know that lots of people are going to be there and that everyone is going to have a great time well into the early morning hours.

You also know that there will be many members of the opposite sex there and you truly want to make an impression. You and your friends are in the mood for some good conversation, lots of laughs, and maybe even some wild and raucous dancing during the night. You definitely want to meet some new guys or some new girls and have a great time (You also need to recover from a certain education professor's brutal mid-term exam.)!

You and your roommates arrive and start checking out the action. You give each person (of the opposite sex) the "once-over" – quickly appraising their attractiveness, beauty/handsomeness, allure, or body language. Your "review" of each person at the party doesn't take very long. You've done this before – in a thousand different social situations from family gatherings to high school classes to shopping excursions. You know what to look for – you're familiar with the patterns, the looks, and the visual appeal that gets your attention (or not).

In other words, you're pretty good at looking at other people for the first time and determining if they are a "YES" ("I'd like to get to know this person a little bit more.") or a "NO" ("I don't think that this person and I have anything in common; I think I'll move on."). You've given each person the six-second once-over!

✓EXTRA CREDIT:

Read each description of a person below (in less than six seconds) and indicate if that individual is a "YES" or a "NO."

1. Wears a paisley shirt with plaid pants. YES NO

2. Wears bright red socks with sandals. YES NO

3. Clothes have excessive wrinkles (just out of the hamper) YES NO

4. An excess of perfume and an abundance of bling YES NO

5. Unwashed hands and dirty fingernails YES NO

Assuming you indicated a "NO" for each of the statements above, then we can also assume you have developed a good way of reading the many people you meet every day. Resume readers have also developed a good sense of the features that attract them…all in six seconds or less.

Aesthetics

Now, let's say you're driving along a city street. As you look around, you may find yourself liking some of the buildings on that street and disliking others. By the same token, when you are in a clothing store there will be some fashions you particularly admire and others that you totally hate. At an art museum there will be some works that absolutely enchant you and others that you could care less about. That's all aesthetics. By definition, aesthetics is the study of beauty and taste. That is to say, how something looks often determines how it is accepted.

Aesthetics also comes into play in the documents we create. For example, when my students turn in papers for course assignments I can get an initial "first impression" based on the aesthetics of each paper submitted. The fonts that are used, whether graphics are included, whether the paper is double or single spaced, the use of any color, or the addition of a cover sheet quickly lets me know if a submission has been done in a professional manner or whether it was done an hour before class. In other words, the "like-ability" of a paper (even before I actually read that paper) influences me when I sit down and actually take the time to read that paper.

The aesthetics of your resume do the same thing. If your resume is "likeable" then it is highly likely that it will get a most favorable review. By the same token, if your resume looks as if it was a hodgepodge of fonts, colors, graphics and other items it may get a less than favorable review. Aesthetics matter! Make your resume look good and your resume will make you look good.

FROM THE PRINCIPAL'S DESK:

"There are many applicants for positions at this time in education. To me, the resume is the catalyst to get an interview, and it is extremely important. That is something I think many teacher candidates miss. They do not put as much value on their resume as they should."

By this point you have probably figured out that an attractive resume will get more positive looks than an unattractive one. Just as important, an attractive resume will send a very positive message to any reader: "This individual respects my time and has presented me with a document I can easily scan and one which offers necessary and critical information in an easy-to-digest format. I like that!"

A TOUCH OF HUMOR

Here's a skill you don't often see, but one a certain candidate thought was appropriate for the position:

"Able to say the ABCs backward in under five seconds."

It's quite one thing to have all your background information recorded on a sheet of paper; quite another to present that information in a physically attractive format and visually appealing design. You want to get your message across, but you also want that message to be presented in a way that will positively attract the attention of an administrator who has an opening in her or his school.

You can ensure the aesthetics of your resume by attending to the following criteria:

- Uniformity
- Symmetry

Let's take a look:

Uniformity

Read the following two sentences. They both have the same exact words, yet one is considerably easier to read than the other:

- He put his hand on the back of her neck and gently pulled her closer.
- He put his hand On the back of her neck and gently pulled her closer.

You, most likely, had some difficulty reading the second sentence simply because there was a lack of uniformity. The letters were of varying sizes, scripts and fonts. From a visual standpoint the second sentence was struggle to read because your eyes had to make constant adjustments as they encountered each of the variations embedded in the words.

Now, for a moment, imagine a resume with a wide variety of sizes, shapes, dimensions, spaces and other typographical irregularities and you can quickly see how frustrating it would be for someone to read. It's quite all right to be creative in your resume design, but please keep in mind that an excess of creativity may do you more harm than good.

FROM THE PRINCIPAL'S DESK:

"I would say that the most common mistake I see on resumes is when candidates get too cute with the layout."

Being consistent in your resume design can make your document more visually appealing while, at the same time, informing the reader that you have a sense of logic, order and purpose. Your resume design sends a powerful message to any reader – one that says you are more interested in meeting their needs than you are in presenting your information in a wildly creative format. Lack of consistency and uniformity in a resume may also reveal an individual with potentially significant deficits in those areas in terms of personality and work habits. For many administrators that would be a serious "red flag."

Here's how to ensure <u>uniformity</u> throughout your resume:

Font Selection

Selection of an appropriate font is critical to the impact you want your resume to make on any reader. Select a fancy and elaborate font (e.g. Brush Script, Clarendon Condensed, Lucida Console) and the message you will be sending to any reader is that you are more concerned with your image than you are with the instructional needs of the administrator reading your document. Fancy fonts have no business in any teacher's resume.

You want to select a font that is familiar, clean, and easy to read. That places a limit on what you can use in a professional resume. Here are the fonts recommended for teacher resumes:

- Arial
- Century
- Courier New
- Georgia
- Tahoma
- Times New Roman

You might want to keep in mind that about 90 percent of all resumes are typed in Times New Roman. There's nothing wrong with that, but you may want to consider alternate typestyles in order to give your readers some "visual relief" – particularly if they're reading scores of resumes.

INSIDER TIP

What is important is not the typestyle you choose, but rather the consistency of typestyle throughout the entire document. In other words, what you don't want to do is to have sixteen different fonts in your resume – you'll be screaming to every reader that you are an amateur, and you'll be causing an enormous strain on somebody's tired old eyes (especially mine). It's perfectly O.K. to use two different fonts in your resume (one for titles, the other for the basic text) – but remember that your goal is to create a document that allows a reader to obtain the important information in an easy-to-read format.

Font Consistency

As you saw in the example above, a wide variety of font styles makes a document (or even a single line of text) that much more difficult to read. Thus, it is extremely important that you use the same font for each and every heading within a resume and for each and every section that appears under those headings. For example, you might select Tahoma for your first heading (Objective) on your resume. If you do, then make sure you select Tahoma for all the other headings as well.

Point Size Consistency

Point size refers to the height of your selected characters (letters or symbols). There are 72 points per inch. Here are a few examples:

- This is 9 point font
- This is 12 point font
- This is 20 point font
- This is 28 point font

If the type size if too small, your resume will be difficult to read and difficult to skim for essential information. An oversized font often conveys a negative impression – a juvenile or unprofessional image.

As a general rule, select a 12-point font. Normally, anything smaller that 12-point will be difficult to skim. Smaller fonts tend to slow down the skimming process simply because they are out of the ordinary – something not normally experienced in most documents read by administrators. A 12-point font is much more comfortable to read. The only exceptions to that rule would be a slightly larger font for your name at the top of the page (16 point is suggested) and a slightly smaller point size for each of the section heading s (14 point is suggested).

Line Space

If you have a two-line space between your first section heading and the text for that section, then you should also have a two-line space between every other section heading and its accompanying text. The spacing between sections should also be consistent throughout the resume.

Type Enhancements

Bold, italics, underlining, and CAPITALIZATION are O.K. to use in order to highlight certain words, phrases, achievements, projects, numbers, and other information to which you want to draw special attention. However, do not overuse these enhancements. If your resume becomes too cluttered, nothing stands out.

Also, keep this in mind – each separate enhancement causes the eyes to slow down just a tiny bit. If there are a lot of enhancements, then that initial six second review of your resume will reveal only a modicum of the information the reader needs in order to make a "YES" or "NO" decision. In short, you may be cheating yourself by forcing the reader to make a decision with less information rather than more.

Bullet styles

In the Paragraph section on the "Home" ribbon of Word 2013 you will find a variety of bullet styles, such as the following:

- Xxx
- o Xxx
- ■ Xxx
- ✓ Xxx
- ➢ Xxx

You are strongly advised to select a single bullet style and then stick to that style throughout the entire resume. Although there are no hard and fast rules about which is the "best" bullet style, most people will agree that the dark round circle (the first item above) is the most common and, thus, the preferred style.

FROM THE PRINCIPAL'S DESK:

"Visually, it is great to see consistent formatting throughout, as this shows a desire to present in a professional way."

Page Length

One page. End of discussion!

White Space

White space is essential to a well-designed resume. Nobody wants to read a document that has text from top to bottom and side to side. That's just way too much visual information. White space – space on the page not covered by type – gives the eyes a chance to rest and properly focus on the essential elements of a document. When there's insufficient white space, the eyes become overloaded with information and tire easily. Too much information is just that – too much information.

White space is common in many print advertisements. The next time you're reading a magazine or looking at a billboard, notice the amount of white space that is used in the ad. It's the number one criteria many graphic designers use when creating advertisements simply because it makes the images and text stand out.

Now, take a look at this book. Notice how there is considerable white space around all four borders. Notice that the text is broken up with indented lists, boxed items (e.g. From the Principal's Desk), double-spacing between paragraphs, and other production values. That white space allows you, the reader, to obtain the greatest amount of information with the least strain on your eyes. So it should be with your resume. Give your words and sentences a chance to work for you – give them room to breathe.

"But, how much white space should I have?" you may be asking. Unfortunately, there's no easy answer to that question because every resume is different and every resume will be designed to convey a singular and individual message. What's important is that your document isn't "text dense" – overflowing with far too many words. Surround those words with stretches of white space. In so doing, the words you use will have more power and more influence – they'll stand out better.

INSIDER TIP

Here's a suggestion that may help you determine if you have sufficient white space on your resume. Tape a copy of your resume to a wall (at eye level) and then step back to a spot where you cannot read the words. Gauge the approximate percentage of white space in relationship to text. If the document appears to be balanced (you followed all the advice in the "Symmetry" section below), then, most likely, you have a good ratio of text to white space.

Paper Color

One choice, and one choice only: white. Please don't make the fatal mistake of typing your resume on any other color. Sure Florescent Orange, Passionate Purple, and Fire Engine Red will get your resume noticed...but for all the wrong reasons. Colored paper literally screams AMATEUR and will surely get your document sent to the nearest "circular file."

FROM THE PRINCIPAL'S DESK:

"If my eyes are bleeding as a result of shock experienced from your use of neon paper, I will probably have traumatic amnesia regarding your bona fides. Try and submit it again on normal paper."

Paper Quality

Use a universal paper stock (20 lb., 8½ x 11) when writing your resume. This is a standard weight and size used throughout the business world and one you should use as well. Use the same paper for cover letters and thank you letters.

Graphics

There seems to be considerable disagreement on this particular issue. Several resume writing books suggest graphics as a way of enhancing a text-heavy document. In addition, teacher sites advocate using graphics as visual "markers" for certain sections of a resume.

I say "NO." No graphics!

In my conversations with principals around the country (you know, the folks who will actually be reading those resumes, instead of just giving advice about writing them) the overwhelming consensus was that the addition of graphics is unprofessional, detracts from the overall message of the resume, is often overdone, is frequently done badly, includes questionable artwork, and adds a certain element of "cuteness" (in this case, "cuteness" is a negative term). A resume is not about your artistic or graphic talents; it is about how your experiences match up with the instructional needs of a school or district.

FROM THE PRINCIPAL'S DESK:

"Big mistake - too many graphics."

Color

Everything I said in the section above also applies to the use of color in your resume. No colored borders! No colored words! No colored graphics. No color – <u>period</u>!

Consistency

Well-structured and well-designed resumes are all about consistency. For example, if you choose to bold a job title, make sure you bold every job title. By the same token, if one of your Qualifications is written in Times New Roman font, then all of your Qualifications should be written in Times New Roman font. The key question here is: What will help a reader get the most amount of information in the shortest amount of time? If there's a lot of variation in your document you will be (visually) slowing the reader down. That's not something you want to do.

Symmetry

For a moment, let's consider a familiar object: A wine glass.

Look at this glass and you will immediately note several things. One, it is perfectly balanced. It doesn't tip to one side or the other – it stands straight and true. Second, it is proportional. If you drew a straight line down the middle of the illustration (from the top of the glass to the bottom) you would create a mirror image – one side looks just like the other, only in reverse. And, third, it is whole. If you were to pour a liquid beverage into this glass it would not leak or lose its contents. The overall image has a powerful message: "I am absolutely complete."

Equally interesting is the fact that a quick glance at this object reveals all its positive features and all its benefits. True, you and I and a hundred million people on this planet would recognize the benefits of this object simply because we have dealt with it (and all its variations) for so many years. We know what to expect from a wine glass and we know how it should perform when a liquid is poured into it. In essence, it is well-balanced, well-proportioned and well designed. It does the job it is supposed to do.

A resume is much like a wine glass. A well-designed one will be balanced, proportional, and highly functional. Wine glasses may come in a wide variety of shapes and sizes, but they are all designed to do one thing and do it well – hold a liquid (wine). Resumes, too, may come in a wide variety of "shapes and sizes," but if they don't do their designated job (effectively advertise the author of that resume), then they may collapse.

You have probably seen a diverse assembly of glassware during your life. Consider for a moment that principals, too, have seen a diverse collection of resumes during their professional careers. With so many variations out there, which one do you think gets their attention more than any other? (Hint: K.I.S.S.).

FROM THE PRINCIPAL'S DESK:

"I like 'clean' looking resumes (neatly arranged and organized)."

Following are some suggestions that will help your resume achieve a sense of symmetry:

Top and Bottom

The visual symmetry of your resume can be achieved by paying attention to the margins at the top and the bottom of your document. Depending on the amount of information you have on a page, there may be some difference in the margin at the top in comparison to the margin at the bottom. For example, you may have a one-inch margin at the top of the page and a .8 inch margin at the bottom. That's O.K. As much as possible, you want your top and bottom margins to be nearly the same. What you don't want is (for example) a one-inch margin at the top and a .3-inch margin at the bottom. As a rule of thumb, I suggest that you try for a .8-inch margin at both the top and bottom of your resume. Try, as much as possible, to get within .3-inch of that standard (at the bottom) as you can.

INSIDER TIP

Print out a draft of your resume and then fold it in thirds (as though you were going to insert it into a #10 business envelope). Open it up and take a close look at the information that is above the first fold (the top third of the resume page). This is the most important part of your resume – the part that is going to make a "first impression" with a reader. At the very least, this section should include your contact data, your objective, and a few qualifications. Make sure this section is visually appealing and packed with impressive data simply because those factors will be an inducement for the reader to scan the remainder of your resume.

Side to Side

You don't want the text of your resume to run from one edge of the paper all the way to the other edge. From a visual standpoint this places an added burden on the eyes to maintain a focus on lines of text that may have as many as 100 characters (e.g. 100 individual letters and spaces per line). Books and published articles typically have between 65 and 70 characters per line and, thus, our eyes are accustomed to that standard. As a rule of thumb, your resume should have a one-inch margin on the left and a one-inch margin on the right. If you use a standard word processing program such as Word 2013, the default setting will be at 65-70 characters per line.

INSIDER TIP

When you complete the first draft of your resume, go through it line by line and note if you have any "orphan words" (single words left on a line by themselves). Edit and revise the previous line (or two) for each one so they can fit. This will tighten up your resume and open up some extra lines for you to add additional information.

Justification

There is no definitive word on whether your resume should have a full justification (the text appears to be inside an invisible box) or a ragged right justification.

Full Justification

This is a short paragraph that has full justification. As you read this paragraph you will notice that all the lines begin at the same vertical line on the left-hand side of this box. You will also notice that all those same lines end at exactly the same place (another invisible line) on the right side of the box. As a result, everything in this paragraph looks evenly spaced. This feature is easily controlled (in Word) in the 'Paragraph" section in the "Home" section of Table Tools.

Ragged Right Justification

Here is another paragraph. Look closely and you will see (just as in the paragraph above) that all the lines begin at the identical place on the left side of this box (at an imaginary vertical line). Yet, on the right side of this paragraph all the lines end at different places. This is due to the different lengths of individual words ("individual" is longer than "words"). As a result, the right side of this piece of text looks uneven or ragged. That's how this block of text got its name – "Ragged Right."

Opinions from many professional resume writers are split on this issue, with no consensus of opinion. Some indicate that a full justification often makes the resume seen more balanced and thus more professional. Others cite evidence that a document with ragged right justification can be read faster than a document with full justification. Conversations with principals does not reveal a preferred method of justification. My suggestion: Ragged right (It's what most people are familiar with since it is used in most documents and books.)

INSIDER TIP

Here's one way to determine if your resume is balanced top to bottom and side to side. Make two copies of your resume. Tape one copy to a wall at eye level. Tape the other copy to the wall, beside the first copy, but turn it upside down. Now, stand back from the two resumes to a point where you cannot read the text. Look carefully at them and see if they appear lopsided or unbalanced. If they do, then you may need to spend a little more time on balancing the text within your document.

The Good, the Bad, and THE UGLY!

You can design your resume in many different ways, but if it doesn't do its intended job, then it becomes less than functional. It becomes dysfunctional. Here's what you need to always keep in mind: A resume is both a textual document as well as a visual one. It's one thing to have all the necessary information in a resume, it's quite another to have that information presented in a pleasing, informative and satisfactory way. A complex resume will do you no favors; a simple one will work to your best advantage.

A TOUCH OF HUMOR

Candidates bring a wealth of skills to any job opening. Here's a talent one candidate thought was particularly important:

"Skills: I can type without looking at the keyboard."

Recall what we shared back in Chapter 2, specifically about the amount of time it takes an experienced administrator to scan a single resume. She or he knows exactly what to look for and their eyes track down a resume scanning for that significant information. If they can't locate the information they know should be there then the resume won't pass this initial and critical first test.

Thus, you want to be sure you provide any reader with the necessary information in the appropriate places. Hiding that information amongst fancy fonts, tucking it into a radical design, or putting it into places it doesn't belong will work to your disadvantage. Remember, your document may only get six seconds of time. If the reader has to work harder than necessary to obtain the data she or he needs, then that six seconds may be wasted. A principal's time is limited, but you can help her or him enormously by focusing on the visual impression.

Now, let's take a look at a resume that is visually flawed ("THE UGLY"):

What's wrong with this resume? Just about everything! Despite having a lack of detail along with several inappropriate entries, this document suffers from a number of visual mistakes. Let's take a look:

- The inconsistent bolding make this resume much too difficult to read.

- The italics are inappropriate and unnecessary.

- The horizontal lines are visually distracting.

- The boxed entries impede a smooth reading.

- There is considerable inconsistency in both the text and the format.

- Bullet points have been used improperly.

- Various fonts are inappropriately used throughout the document.

- OMG – Clip art!

Suffice it to say, this document would try the patience of even the most seasoned resume reader. Instead of a professional document, it screams "amateur" at every turn. I doubt it would garner even six seconds of reading time. Its visual confusion and graphic muddling would, most assuredly, propel it towards the nearest trash can!

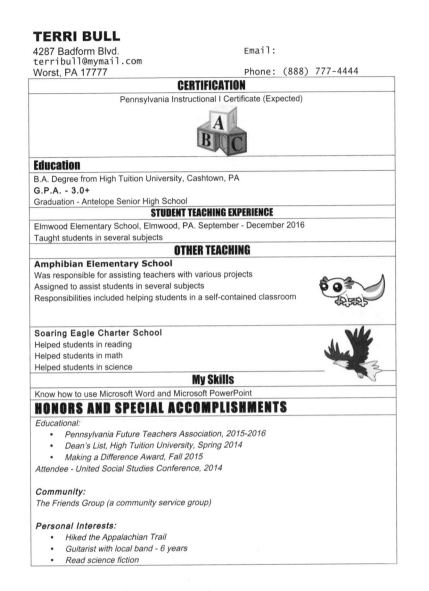

TERRI BULL

4287 Badform Blvd.
terribull@mymail.com
Worst, PA 17777

Email:

Phone: (888) 777-4444

CERTIFICATION

Pennsylvania Instructional I Certificate (Expected)

Education

B.A. Degree from High Tuition University, Cashtown, PA

G.P.A. - 3.0+

Graduation - Antelope Senior High School

STUDENT TEACHING EXPERIENCE

Elmwood Elementary School, Elmwood, PA. September - December 2016

Taught students in several subjects

OTHER TEACHING

Amphibian Elementary School

Was responsible for assisting teachers with various projects

Assigned to assist students in several subjects

Responsibilities included helping students in a self-contained classroom

Soaring Eagle Charter School

Helped students in reading

Helped students in math

Helped students in science

My Skills

Know how to use Microsoft Word and Microsoft PowerPoint

HONORS AND SPECIAL ACCOMPLISHMENTS

Educational:
- *Pennsylvania Future Teachers Association, 2015-2016*
- *Dean's List, High Tuition University, Spring 2014*
- *Making a Difference Award, Fall 2015*

Attendee - United Social Studies Conference, 2014

Community:
The Friends Group (a community service group)

Personal Interests:
- *Hiked the Appalachian Trail*
- *Guitarist with local band - 6 years*
- *Read science fiction*

FROM THE PRINCIPAL'S DESK:

"One of the most common mistakes made by teacher candidates is adding clip art or other kinds of pictures. For example, a resume that has the alphabet blocks (A, B, C) is an immediate rejection for me."

As you probably noted, all the information in this document was buried under an avalanche of lines, boxes, fancy fonts, capital letters, and crazy designs such that it was virtually impossible to decipher. Like me, your eyes were probably all over the pages – dancing left to right and right to left in a constant search for information. To put it mildly it was a frustrating (and tiring) experience to read this resume. You and I were both visually exhausted and couldn't wait to move on to something else. This is definitely not what you want to do!

* * *

In the course of my research for this book I read through dozens of professional resume books. What I saw was a wide diversity of resume formats from the elaborate to the simplistic. I also took the opportunity to speak with career counselors at several colleges to get their insights and advice. They, too, provided me with a range of resume samples and resume formats – again from complex to simple. I also contacted several professional resume writers to get their insights and suggestions. There were lots of opinions, but very few rules. It seemed that everyone with an ounce of advice on writing resumes had a somewhat different perspective on what a good resume should look like.

So, I decided to take my research directly to the people who actually read teacher resumes…your resume, specifically. I talked to elementary, middle school, and secondary principals and asked them what they would most like to see in a well-designed resume. While there were a few very minor variations, the basic format suggested in this chapter was the consensus of opinion. It was, as one principal told me, "A very attractive way to present the essential information I need to make a 'Yes' or 'No' decision on a candidate."

But, that's not to say that the format shared here can't be modified or amended to suit your specific experiences or distinctive skills. You'll see some of those modifications throughout the pages of this book. While each modification is slightly different from every other one, you will quickly see that they all adhere to a principle of simplicity that allows a reader (a school administrator) to 1) get a maximum of information in a minimum of time, and 2) be sold (not told) that you are a potential new teacher of both merit and promise.

FROM THE PRINCIPAL'S DESK:

"I'm most impressed by a resume that's professionally done, easy to follow, and possesses clarity."

Chapter 12

Titanic Mistakes That Will Sink You

This book was written to ensure that each and every resume you send out will be, not only a true reflection of who you are as a future teacher, but will also be your ticket to an engaging and successful interview and the teaching job of your dreams. To make sure you had the most up-to-date information I surveyed and interviewed various school administrators across the United States, communicated with superintendents and principals in more than three dozen states, e-mailed and chatted with professional recruiters in a wide variety of businesses and professional enterprises, and tapped into the collective wisdom of many successful teachers who have been through the process before you. What has resulted is a collective tome of the best advice and best recommendations to be found anywhere – an assembly of facts that can and will ensure that your resume will be a standout one.

A significant portion of the research for this book was devoted to the common mistakes and frequent blunders that pre-service teachers often make on their resumes. These are miscues that often doomed their chances, cost them a chance for an interview, or propelled their resume into a principal's wastebasket. These are the mistakes that pop up often enough that they deserve their own chapter. These errors happen so frequently and appear on so many teacher resumes that even many of the most highly qualified candidates never make it to the next stage of the application process. These are the mistakes you want to avoid at all costs – simply because they will infect your resume, pollute your application, and spoil any chances you have of securing an interview.

INSIDER TIP

According to several professional recruiters, and many building principals, more than 80% of all teacher resumes evidence one or more of the following errors – miscues and mistakes that result in those resumes being immediately rejected, discarded or tossed.

As you review this list of common resume blunders I'd like you to keep one critical fact in mind. These mistakes are being made every day by teacher candidates. Many of your competitors for a teaching job will include these errors in their resume, thus ensuring that those documents will be quickly deposited into the nearest trash can. You, on the other hand, can stand out and stand above your completion by ensuring that not a single one of these common errors ever finds its way into your document. If you do that, I can assure you that your resume will rise to the top of any applicant pool. I can also assure you that your resume will signal you as a teacher candidate who takes the time to do things right. And, after all, isn't that what this whole process is about?

1. Three Words: Spelling, Spelling, Spelling

Why do you think "Spelling" is the #1 item on this list of common mistakes? Simply because it is the most common mistake to show up on teacher resumes. Hey, look, you're about to complete four years of college. You've taken at least two English or Writing courses, you've written an endless array of class papers, and you're about to complete at least one semester of student teaching serving as an academic role model for students. Let's face it – spelling counts. In my college courses, if a student submits a paper with more than two spelling errors it gets sent back for a "do-over." No excuses! The hidden message here is that if a teacher candidate doesn't take the time or make the effort to take care of the "little things" (like spelling), how will they ever be able to take care of the "big things" (like teaching kids)? ALWAYS double-check, triple-check, quadruple-check, quintuple-check…your spelling. Trust me, a misspelled word is the first thing a reader will notice on your resume – and the first thing that will send that resume into the trash bin. Spell it. Right.

FROM THE PRINCIPAL'S DESK:

"When hiring for positions we know will generate a lot of applicants (such as Kindergarten positions), we must screen in a very logical way. If we read every resume we received it would take years. So, we look for spelling first – that's a sure indicator."

2. Three More Words: Grammar, Grammar, Grammar

O.K. here's comes the #2 item on our list. Yup, inappropriate grammar is another major virus that frequently contaminates far too many resumes. Make an effort to visit the college writing center, schedule an appointment with someone in the English Department, invite one of your favorite Education professors to review your language, or ask a professional writer in your community for some advice. You can't wimp out on this – improper grammar will automatically jump out and visually attack any reader ensuring your resume a one-way trip to the "NO" pile.

Here are ten of the most common grammar mistakes:

- *Your vs. You're*
- *There vs. They're vs. Their*
- *Its* vs. *It's*
- Passive voice
- Dangling modifiers
- Possessive nouns
- *Affect* vs. *Effect*
- *Me* vs. *I*
- *i.e.* vs. *e.g.*
- *Who* vs. *That*

FROM THE PRINCIPAL'S DESK:

"You would be amazed at the number of resumes I receive that contain multiple spelling and/or grammatical mistakes. When I have 150 applicants for a position, this quickly eliminates them from any consideration."

3. Too Long

Whenever I talk with prospective graduates and ask them for the single most important question they have about resumes, the queries are always the same: "How long should it be?" The following chart answers that question once and for all:

If you are...	...then your resume should be...
A soon to be college graduate about to complete your student teaching semester (and with no prior teaching experience)	From 1 to 1¼ pages long (a single page is the preferred)
A non-traditional soon-to-be college graduate (an older adult student who has returned to college to obtain a teaching certificate)	From 1 to 1½ pages long
An experienced teacher (2+ years of teaching experience) who is changing schools or districts	From 1½ to 2 pages long

Oh please, don't make the fatal mistake one prospective teacher in Ohio made. In order to get all the information on his 1-page resume he wrote it all in 9-point font. Bad idea!

4. Clip Art

One word: No, No, NO! (O.K., that was three words, but I really wanted to make my point!). Your resume needs to be professional, not cute. "Cute" won't get you an interview; "Professional" will.

5. Not Customizing the Resume

If you send me a letter personalized with my name and other information specific to me I can assure you it will get my undivided attention. Send me something generic ("Dear Occupant:") and I'll, most likely, treat it as junk mail – ensuring that its journey from my hand to the trash can will be swift and deliberate. Bottom line: Each resume MUST BE customized for a particular reader at a particular institution. Generic letters will always get a generic response: "No thanks!"

6. Too Much Clutter

If you have a variety of fonts, lots of lines going back and forth, a few examples of clip art, lots of colored type, overuse of caps and bolding, excessive underlining and a plethora of symbols such as arrows, emojis, and other symbols it is certain your resume will stand out...but, for all the wrong reasons. Lots of visual clutter on your resume sends a message to the reader that you are either not entirely serious about the position you're applying for or that you are trying to cover something up with sparkle and flash. Neither impression will get you into the "Yes" pile, and will, most definitely, doom any chance you may have had for an interview. If you want to demonstrate your creative skills I would suggest you save them for another project and another document not related to your job search.

7. Inappropriate Formatting

Oh please, re-read Chapter 11 one more time (Please, please, please!). Principals have had their fill of oversized and inappropriate fonts, boxes scattered across the page, an abundance of horizontal and vertical lines, unnecessary categories ("Very Dear People Who Have Inspired and Motivated Me to be The Next Really Exceptional Teacher"), colored typefaces, and artwork scattered around the borders of applicant resumes.

INSIDER TIP

Make sure your formatting is consistent across your resume. That is, all headers are in the same style, all indentations line up, all the bullets are similar, etc. Consistency will help ensure that a busy administrator will gather as much information as possible during the initial scan.

8. Copy and Paste

Your college's career center probably has several examples of appropriate resumes or even some templates to help you build your own resume. Read those, but never copy them. If you try to create a "cut and paste" resume you will be driving a long sharp knife into your efforts. One, it's very easy to tell if your resume was created from the scraps and detritus of other resumes. Two, the language will be choppy and not reflective of your unique writing style. And, three, you may be doing something that many other applicants do (in order to save time) – something that will be quickly and easily recognized by anyone reading those resumes. Worst of all, you will wind up with a most unprofessional document.

9. Uses an Inappropriate E-mail Address

I know, all through college you've been using really cool email addresses such as studmonster@XXXX.net, beerpong33@XXXX. net, partygirl21@XXXX.net, and babe-a-licious@XXXX.net to communicate with your friends. But, don't even think about using racy, inappropriate, silly, or totally unprofessional email addresses on your resume. Trust me, this will get you kicked into the "NO" pile faster than anything else. Set up a professional email account (e.g. Bobcanter22@...., HeatherH@....) through Gmail, Hotmail, or Yahoo – all of which are free. In fact, I would suggest setting up (and using) those emails at least 5-6 months in advance of graduation so that they are a natural part of your communication and outreach efforts.

INSIDER TIP

Don't use or list your .edu email address on any resume. If your college is like mine, those addresses are frequently deleted from the institution's files after people graduate. If you are selected for an interview (after graduation) as a result of your resume and the principal sends a message to your .edu email you may never get it (the principal will get a reply that the message was "undeliverable"). Set up and use a Gmail account (for example) and you can be sure that administrators will be able to contact you - no matter what time of year.

FROM THE PRINCIPAL'S DESK:

"Do not use 'cutesy' email addresses on your professional resume. hellokitty@... is not a professional contact."

10. Uses a Long-winded and Meaningless Objective

Go back and read Chapter 7. Please.

11. Neglects Certification

If you are applying for a specific position, a principal needs to know that you are (or will be) appropriately certified for that position. If there is any doubt in her or his mind about whether you have (or will have) the necessary teaching certificate, then it is highly likely that your application will find its way into the "NO" pile. Don't leave any doubt – make sure it is listed on your resume. Triple-check this one.

12. A Photo of Yourself

I apologize in advance if I step on your ego with this piece of advice, but your looks will have nothing to do with your success in obtaining a teaching position. Principals aren't concerned with putting together a good looking faculty, they are more interested in assembling the best qualified faculty who can address the academic needs of all students. Submitting a photo won't be part of the decision-making process. In short, your face won't get you an interview, but your talents and desire will! Post all your "selfies" on Facebook, don't include any of them with your resume.

FROM THE PRINCIPAL'S DESK:

"Don't include photographs or glamour shots. I'm not going to hire you based on your good looks."

Oh, elementary teachers, photos of your clearly creative classroom projects, wonderfully dynamic bulletin boards, and absolutely unique room arrangements are also unnecessary and inappropriate. Those should be posted on Pinterest, not included with your application.

13. Repeat Information from the Cover Letter

As you will discover in the next section of this book, your cover letter should be written to compliment the data included on your resume. Administrators look at your resume to determine if you have the requisite skills, experiences, and qualifications specific to an advertised position. Your cover letter confirms that initial impression.

14. Not Sufficiently Addressing Your Achievements

In my conversations with administrators from around the country I often asked them about what makes a good achievement; that is, what is it about an 'achievement' that makes it stand out, or stand apart from the "same old, same old." The advice I received can be boiled down into three critical criteria. In other words, list 'achievements' only if and when they satisfy each and every one of these standards;

- ✓ Is it something you are proud of? Did you make a difference in a child's life? Did you change someone's attitude or help them become a better learner? Did you contribute to an improvement in learning in some marked way?

- ✓ Is it education-related? Is there some connection to what is normally done in a formal classroom environment? Was something taught; was something learned? Did it touch on a topic or subject normally shared in an elementary, middle school, or secondary environment?

- ✓ Can you defend it verbally? Is it something you would be willing or excited to share in a formal interview? Is it something you would discuss with one of your professors or in one of your courses?

15. Includes Experiences Unrelated to Teaching

You are the undisputed "foosball" champion in your fraternity. Terrific! You held three part-time jobs last summer at the beach. Incredible! Your impression of Beyoncé at *The Daily Dive* last Friday night got a standing round of applause. Amazing! It's just that all that stuff (totally unrelated to education) would be inappropriate to include on your resume. If you have an experience that demonstrates direct contact with school-age children, then include it on your resume. Otherwise, you just might want to keep it to yourself.

16. Your Hobbies

Your hobbies, unless they are directly related to classroom work, should be excluded from your resume. The fact that you are a champion tap dancer, world class motorcycle mechanic, or up and coming tattoo artist does not advance your talents as a future educator. For the most part, your hobbies should not be included on your resume.

There are times, however, when your hobbies (especially if they are education-related) can be a positive addition to your resume. Look at the following examples and you'll see what I mean:

- Organized and maintained an after-school stamp collecting club focused on the stamps of Africa – a program that was successfully incorporated into the 12th grade geography curriculum.

- Constructed a model railroad layout in the classroom that demonstrated the advance of the western frontier in the 1800s. A time-lapse video of the six-week project was instrumental in improved mid-term scores in American History.

- Demonstrated the evolution of cameras in a unit on 20th and 21st century technology that resulted in improved attitudes about the role of technology as a "change agent" in American social institutions.

A TOUCH OF HUMOR

Here's an interesting pastime included on one person's resume:

"Hobbies: Enjoy cooking Chinese and Italians."

17. Dumps Lots of Flowery Adjectives into the Resume

"I am a conscientious, dependable, dedicated, enthusiastic, dynamic, innovative, outgoing, and self-reliant teacher who is also logical, diligent, objective, resourceful, confident, and blah, blah, blah..." Here's a person who is so full of himself that there is absolutely no way any administrator is going to bring him in for an interview. His over-inflated ego would fill the room so much that it would result in some serious structural damage. Put the emphasis on verbs, not flowery (and self-serving) adjectives.

18. Lists Every Accomplishment since Elementary School

The fact that you won the 60-yard dash at the fifth grade annual track meet or that you were the assistant captain of your 10th grade debate team is certainly laudable. But don't include that information on your resume. Only include what you have done during your college years – the years in which you have systematically prepared yourself for a teaching career. Anything before those college experiences will make your resume seem "padded" – filled with a mass of ancient data that adds lots of words, but not lots of current educational experiences. Short story: only include educationally-related college experiences.

19. Any Unnecessary, Obvious Words, like "Phone"

Trust me, if you include something like (777) 555-1234 under your name at the top of your resume, I'm pretty sure it is your phone number. You really don't have to identify it as "PHONE: (777) 555-1234". By the same token, if you include something like marysmith@ZZZZ.com on your resume I should be able to figure out that it is an email address. Yeah, I'm pretty old, but it's really not necessary to identify those contacts for me. Thanks anyway!

INSIDER TIP

If you are tight for space, select a font in which the letters are more closely packed together. For example, look at the following six instances of the phrase "research results illustrated":

Research results illustrated

Research results illustrated

Research results illustrated

Research results illustrated

Research results illustrated

Research results illustrated

You will note that the third item (which used a Courier New font) took up more line space than did the last item (which used a Times New Roman font). The second item (Century font) used slightly more line space than did the fifth item (Tahoma font). Choose your font carefully and you can create more space for all your information.

---

21. Uses Colored Font and/or Colored Paper

Two words: black & white (black type, white paper)

Oh, two more words: No exceptions!

FROM THE PRINCIPAL'S DESK:

"Really long resumes, those with colored paper, and those with a scent will quickly get discarded. Simple is always best."

22. Way Too Much Text

When you try to cram a plethora of information onto a resume page by using a .4 inch margin and a 9-point font size (see above), you are taxing both the principal's patience as well as eyesight. You are always safe with a 1-inch margin all around and a 12-point font size. Consider some serious editing and some serious prioritizing to keep your resume to traditional limits (see #3 above).

23. Unrelated Social Media URLs

Links to your Instagram account, Pinterest page, Facebook, or opinionated blogs are always inappropriate. Principals aren't interested in what you think about your favorite sports team, the grade you got on your World Geography mid-term exam, or some of the activities you participated in over Semester Break. On the other hand, do list professional URLs such as a relevant LinkedIn page or personal (and professional) web site. Such sites can often give your resume added value by offering additional information about who you are and what you bring to the education profession.

24. Sorry, But it Needs Repeating: Spelling, Spelling, Spelling

How would you feel if, while reading this book, you discovered three or four spelling mistakes on every page? You would, most likely, feel disrespected or cheated. Perhaps you'd feel like the author was a total idiot for not taking the time to make sure every single word was spelled correctly. You might even feel as though you had been scammed out of your money for a book rife with an incredible number of spelling errors. Your feelings about a book overflowing with spelling mistakes is often what principals feel when reading resumes containing an abundance of mis-spellings. Take the time. **Please** take the time. It <u>DOES</u> make a difference!

FROM THE PRINCIPAL'S DESK:

"Spelling mistakes on resumes will automatically put them on the 'NO' pile."

INSIDER TIP

You can easily create your own personal and professional web site on <u>www.wix.com</u> of <u>www.weebly.com</u>. These easy to use sites give you lots of assistance in creating a free site with an array of innovative tools, templates, and lots of online support. A personal web site would be a great place to showcase lesson plans, classroom designs, an art portfolio, or videos of classroom lessons. If you create a site, be sure it is featured in the contact information at the top of your resume.

25. Uses a Template from the Career Center

Bad move! Most of the templates available from your college's career center are too generic. Many of them are, most likely, not specific enough to the education profession. If a principal sees too many resumes that look like they have come from the same resource, then it is highly likely that all those resumes will suffer the same fate: "Thanks, but no thanks!" I know you don't want to hear this, but it's always advisable to write your resume from scratch. That way, you can make it unique, singular, and distinctive. Yes, it's more work, but that work might just pay off in a job interview (while everyone else continues to send out their "same old, same old" resumes).

26. Personal Stuff

Do not include information about any of the following on your resume:

- Birth date or age
- Marital status
- Religion
- Physical disabilities
- Sexual orientation
- Medical history
- Parents' occupations
- Country of origin
- Living arrangements
- Bodily adornments
- Legal challenges
- Political affiliations
- Native language
- Debt history

It is illegal for employers to ask for the information listed above AND it is also illegal for an employer to use any of the information above in making a hiring decision. You should be hired based on your abilities and aptitude; not on your religion, sexual orientation, cultural background, political beliefs, or really cool tattoos.

27. Writes Boastfully

Write with confidence, not with arrogance. Let the reader know you are accomplished, talented, and skilled in the various responsibilities associated with classroom teaching. Don't make the mistake, however, of assuming that you are the only one (or the best one) with those attributes. If you go back and re-read the section in Chapter 9 about how to write a great experience (bullet point), you'll note that I strongly suggested the elimination of the words "I" and "me." By getting rid of those words, and beginning each of the experiential bullet points with a strong verb instead, you will have effectively moved from any sense of arrogance and ensured that the emphasis is now on your talents...and not your ego.

INSIDER TIP

Go through your resume and eliminate as many instances of "I" or "Me" as you can. Those two words are often "red flags" for principals - a signal that the writer is more interested in herself or himself than they are in contributing to the academic welfare of the school. You will strengthen your resume considerably with a reduction of those words whenever possible.

---

28. Opinions, Not Facts

O.K., very short quiz: You're the principal of a school. Which of the following two people would you be most likely to hire?

- I think I'm really a very personable individual and I believe I am someone who is way easy to work within a big organization, like in a school.

- Participated actively and enthusiastically in staff meetings to address community concerns, parent involvement, and new grading procedures for all fourth grade students at Dandelion Elementary School.

There are three phrases you need to eliminate from your resume (and cover letter) now and forever: "I believe", "I feel" and "I think." Principals want to know what you've done, not what you (or anyone else) thinks or believes you might be able to do in the future.

29. Overuse of Educational Buzzwords

I'm sure you know some of the most common phrases and buzzwords used throughout the education profession. You've seen these terms in your textbooks, heard them in class lectures, and studied them in preparation for course quizzes and exams. It's quite all right to use some of these terms, but not to an excess. Be careful of "dropping" too many into your resume. You won't impress anyone. Here are a few of the most frequently used terms; use them with caution:

- Common Core Standards
- Cooperative Learning
- Differentiated Instruction
- Higher Order Thinking Skills
- Individual Learning Styles
- Instructional Scaffolding
- Integration of Technology
- Peer Assessment
- Student Progress Monitoring
- Text Complexity

30. Lying

One word: Don't.[1]

31. References

Including a statement like "References available upon request" is very outdated and old-fashioned. And, you're not old fashioned, are you? If you are invited for an interview, the principal will ask you to submit either the names of references or actual letters of recommendation. There's no need to inform the principal (on your resume) that you have them; she or he will assume that you do.

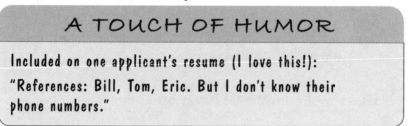

A TOUCH OF HUMOR

Included on one applicant's resume (I love this!):
"References: Bill, Tom, Eric. But I don't know their phone numbers."

---

1 A 2003 study conducted by the Society of Human Resources found that 53% of all job applications contained inaccurate information. A congressional study conducted in 1992 found that one-third of all job applicants fake their resumes or include at least one inaccurate statement. A 2003 study cited by the *The CPA Journal* referenced a survey of 2.6 million job applicants which showed that 44% lied about prior work experience.

Chapter 13

Your Resume Checklist

The following checklist offers you an opportunity to review all the elements of a good resume. You are encouraged to use this document for each and every resume you write. Please make several copies of this list and keep them on hand. Before you send any resume via e-mail or through the mail, you should take the time to check off the items here. Or, as an alternate strategy, you can give your resume and this list to a friend and ask her or him to do the check for you. She or he may see some items (you could easily miss) that need additional attention. In any case, the review should be a regular part of your resume writing agenda.

Overall

❏ An appropriate font was selected (**Arial**, Century, Courier New, **Georgia**, **Tahoma**, Times New Roman).

❏ The font is consistent throughout the document.

❏ The point size of the font is consistent throughout the resume.

❏ There are appropriate spacings between lines and blocks of text.

❏ **Bold**, <u>underline</u>, and *italics* are used judiciously and sparingly.

❏ My choice of bullet styles is appropriate and consistent throughout the document.

❏ There is sufficient white space all around the resume.

❏ The overall document is one that *sells*, rather than one that *tells*.

❏ The document is of an appropriate length (approximately 1 page).

❏ The resume is printed on white paper.

❏ The paper chosen is of a standard weight (20#).

❏ There are no graphics or art work on the resume.

❏ Black ink has been used throughout the document.

❏ All spelling is correct and has been checked several times.

❏ The grammar is correct and has been checked several times.

❏ There is absolutely no"cute" formatting anywhere in the document.

❏ I have not included any personal opinions; facts only.

Contact Data

❏ My name has been bolded and set in a larger font at the top of the page.

❏ I have provided any necessary pronunciation clues.

❏ I have provided an appropriate mailing address.

❏ I have included one or more telephone numbers where I can be easily reached.

❏ I have provided a professional e-mail address.

❏ As appropriate, I have included "extra" contact information.

Objective

❏ My objective is short, sweet, and simple (K.I.S.S.).

❏ My objective is not filled with "puffy" words or hackneyed jargon.

❏ My objective is tailored for the specific position advertised.

Qualifications

❏ My personal profile is succinct, accurate, and brief.

❏ I have distinguished myself as an excellent teacher.

❏ I have written my Personal Profile in paragraph form.

❏ I have demonstrated a match between my Objective and my Qualifications.

Education and Certification

❏ I have listed my degree(s) or anticipated degree(s).

❏ I have listed my certification (or anticipated certification).

❏ I have demonstrated a match between my Objective and my Certification.

Professional Teaching Experiences

❏ All statements begin with an action verb.

❏ All verbs are in the same tense (past or present).

❏ Only information relevant to the position is included.

❏ I have included information on areas of interest specific to the designated school/district.

❏ I have described my experiences, skills, and talents related to the job.

❏ I have not used any personal pronouns.

❏ I have used bullet points in an appropriate manner.

❏ I have placed an emphasis on selling, not telling.

❏ I have limited the use of any "buzz words" or "buzz phrases."

❏ I did not include "References available upon request."

❏ I have included information and wording that make me stand out from other candidates.

Related Experiences

❏ I have listed other specific skills pertinent to the position.

❏ I have included any special public speaking appearances (as appropriate).

❏ I have listed any publications authored or co-authored (as appropriate).

❏ I have listed all honors, awards, and special commendations (as appropriate).

❏ I have included any professional affiliations (as appropriate).

❏ I have listed any community activities in which I am involved (as appropriate).

❏ I have included any coaching experiences (as appropriate).

❏ I have grouped my related experiences in an appropriate manner.

Visual Impression

❏ I have focused my attention on the <u>uniformity</u> of my document.

❏ I have focused my attention of the <u>symmetry</u> of my document.

A TOUCH OF HUMOR

Here's a clear example of why you need to review your resume several times before sending it out:

"Skills: Strong Work Ethic, Attention to Detail, Team Player, Self-Motivated, Attention to Detail."

Chapter 14

<u>Sample Resumes</u>

The following samples illustrate all of the essential ingredients of a good resume. They are provided as examples of what you should do in constructing your own resume(s). Please, don't make the fatal mistake of copying these resumes and using them as your own. By the same token, don't mistakenly use these as all-purpose templates for your documents. Consider that thousands of other potential teachers will be reading this book and if a certain school administrator gets lots of resumes that look similar in design and composition, then she or he may be inclined to reject all of them. These are samples...nothing more. The key to success is to craft your own unique and singular resume – one that could not and should not be duplicated by anyone else.

(Mr.) Haiping Yuan

57 Seaview Lane, Long Beach, WA 98631
(360) 555-8765 (C) • (360) 555-4321 (H)
hyuan@xxx.net

Objective:	Second Grade Teacher
Qualifications:	Sincere and devoted elementary teacher with extensive experience in working with below-level readers. Trained in Reading Recovery and am a teacher committed to the literacy success of all learners. Employs a variety of instructional strategies geared to individual student needs including multiple intelligence instruction, critical thinking opportunities, and active problem-solving. "Haiping is the penultimate teacher – one filled with a plethora of imagination, a dedication to service, and an orientation to student success that signals him as an educator of both promise and passion." - Dr. Constance P. Furman, Professor of Education, Studyhard State College.
Education & Certification	Bachelor of Arts, Elementary Education, Studyhard State College (Expected May 15, 20__). State of Washington, Elementary Education Certification, Grades K-6.

Professional Teaching Experiences

Bivalve Elementary School, Tacoma, WA   Spring 20__
Student Teacher (1st Grade)
- Taught a first grade math unit on numeration that resulted in a 21% increase in math scores on the CTBS.
- Designed a theme-based first grade curriculum focused on self-concept and personality development. Was awarded one of two mini-grants from the Clam Bay PTO to expand the project.
- Developed and taught a series of Nearpod lessons on "Simple Machines" now integrated into the entire K-1 science curriculum.
- Created an integrated literature unit on "Famous Authors" resulting in a 16% improvement in book distribution in the school library.

Shellfish Elementary School, Shelton, WA   Fall 20__
Field Experience (2nd Grade)
- Integrated technology into the 2nd grade language arts curriculum through the use of podcasts and Skype interviews with a Pennsylvania children's author.
- Administered and reviewed the Diagnostic Assessments of Reading (DAR) to 11 students. Implemented appropriate intervention strategies in concert with reading specialist.

Professional Profile

Affiliations
- Washington State Literacy Council
- Elementary Education Association (Tacoma Group)

Honors and Awards
- Distinguished Student Teacher - 20__
- Dean's List - 20__ to Present
- Phi Delta Phi Honor Society - 20__

Special Skills
- Volunteer, Big Brother Organization, Tacoma, WA
- Volunteer, Special Olympics, Bremerton, WA
- Volunteer, Clamtown (WA) Public Library - Storytime reader

Here's a very clean resume. Note how the applicant listed the essential categories down the left side of the document and then provided the necessary information in a compact form. This would be an easy-to-read resume for any busy school administrator.

Crystal Ware 12000 Bayside Village   Galveston, TX 77551
Cell: 409-555-8989   Home: 409-555-7676   Crystalware@xxx.net

12th Grade American History Teacher

Dynamic and engaging professional dedicated to proving a quality-based classroom experience for a diversity of learners... Thorough knowledge of "Best Practices' in history education, particularly for low achieving students... Excellent classroom management skills... Exceptional communication skills - dedicated team player... Recognized by the Texas Historical Society as "an educator filled with a passionate desire to know more, infused with a determination to contribute to the academic success of all students, and possessed of outstanding leadership abilities that are both focused and intense."

Education

Bachelor of Arts, Secondary Education - History, Sandpiper University (May 20___).

Certification

State of Texas - 7-12 History

Professional Teaching Experiences

Hurricane Senior High School - Hurricane, TX   Spring 20___
Student Teacher - 11th Grade

- Developed class web page to encourage more interactive experiences with historical documents. Site is now regular element of overall history curriculum.
- Created and taught two elective mini-courses (The Underground Railroad; After the (Civil) War). Enrollment in each course increased 19-24%.
- Collaborated with other history teachers to implement more technology into the curriculum. These included virtual field trips and numerous Nearpod experiences.
- Managed an after-school tutoring program for struggling students. Participants experienced a 23% improvement state exams (over previous year results).

Tornado High School - Tornado, TX   Fall 20___
Field Experience - 10th Grade

- Prepared and conducted twice-weekly instructional workshops to assist students in passing American History courses.
- Developed a new segment (The Aftermath of Wars) of the American History curriculum as an element of the Gifted Education Initiative.
- Initiated and taught an in-service program for Tornado High School history teachers on "History as Storytelling." Received an overall rating of 6.7 (7-point scale) from faculty.

Testimonials

"Dynamic presenter. Crystal certainly knows how to get everyone engaged." - Dr. Randall Macon, S.U. Dept. of Education.

"Crystal's energy and love for teaching was clearly displayed throughout her student teaching experience." - Mr. Tyrone Williams, History Department, Hurricane High School.

"I thoroughly enjoyed Crystal's lessons. She is full of energy and I was captivated by her classroom management skills, individualized attention, and incredible storytelling ability." - Mr. Douglas Fenstermacher, Principal, Hurricane High School.

This applicant has added some testimonials at the end of her resume. This demonstrates to any reader that others have verified her expertise and teaching abilities. Also note that her philosophy (12th Grade American History Teacher) is positioned in the top third of the document (the part that usually appears above the first fold in a tri-folded letter). This would be the first thing a reader would encounter - a good move!

Dan Saul Knight

769 Newark Avenue
Bloomfield, NJ 07003

www.webportfolio.com

dansaul@xxx.net
862-555-0099

Secondary Art Teacher

Dedicated and determined teacher eager to help students appreciate the arts in their overall education. Eager to change misperceptions about the role of art in everyday life and imbue students with both an appreciation and commitment to art in a comprehensive education. Uses creativity and innovation to motivate students and to expand their learning potential. Possess strong interpersonal skills, eager to work with a team of equally dedicated teachers, and skilled in classroom management techniques that empower students to achieve and succeed.

Education and Certification

- Bachelor of Arts degree in Art Education, New Jersey Northern College, Newark, NJ (Dec. 20__) • GPA: 3.89 • Dean's List (7 semesters)
- New Jersey State Art Certification K-12 (pending)

Professional Teaching Experience

Student Teaching
Bloomfield Senior High School • Bloomfield, NJ (Fall 20__)
- Designed and implemented highly-rated lesson plans focused on individual achievement and personal appreciation.
- Created and taught mini-units on sculpture, studio art, painting, and drawing resulting in improved attitudes towards art by 57% of student body.
- Incorporated art history and art appreciation into all lesson plans. Cooperating teacher commented, "These were some of the most well-conceived and well-received lessons I've ever seen from a student teacher."
- Created a series of Prezis focused on great modern artists. Was also able to incorporate other forms of technology into the overall art curriculum. Comment from building principal: "Dan demonstrates an incredible grasp of art education through his innovative, creative, and dynamic lesson plans."

Field Experiences
Bloomfield Middle School • Bloomfield, NJ (Spring 20__)
- Incorporated language arts strategies into all lesson plans through an interactive relationship with two language arts teachers. Students' language arts scores showed an improvement of 29% over previous year.
- Established the "Art of the Week" project which introduced students to great works of art via regularly broadcast videos on the school channel.

West Orange High School • West Orange, NJ (Fall 20__)
- Developed and incorporated "multiple intelligences" throughout the art curriculum in order to improve both participation and engagement.
- Co-directed with the art teacher a virtual field trip experience that "toured" the studios of contemporary artists. Invited to share this venture at the New Jersey Educator's Conference in Trenton, NJ (November 20__).

Related Experiences

- Visiting artist, Northern New Jersey Art Consortium
- Volunteer "Feature Artist" - Bloomfield Public Library
- Girl Scouts - Brownie Leader (Troop #564)
- Bloomfield Public Library - storyteller for preschool group
- Salvation Army - tutor for ELL students
- Speaker, Chamber of Commerce - "Art Education is for Everyone…Including You!"

The use of bullets in this resume makes it very easy for a reader to locate necessary information. She or he can visually move down the left side of the document and get a clear impression of this applicant in a very short amount of time.

Connie M. Paxton

--9276 Tappen Lane, Kingman, AZ 86402
conniem@xxx.net • 929-555-5678 (C)

OBJECTIVE: Fourth Grade Classroom Teacher

QUALIFICATIONS: Energetic and dedicated teacher with a solid background in child development, classroom management, and invitational education. Experienced with the most up-to-date technology and have implemented innovative and cutting-edge lessons that have engaged students in multiple ways. Excellent knowledge of the instructional needs of struggling students coupled with the skills necessary to ensure their academic success. Devoted to self-improvement - believing that all teachers have room to grow in multiple ways.

- Authentic assessment
- Technology integration
- Differentiated classroom
- Character education
- Enrichment programs
- Curriculum mapping

EDUCATION: Bachelor of Arts, Elementary Education - High Desert College
Certification - Elementary Education Teacher (K-6)

STUDENT TEACHING: Ponderosa Elementary School, Flagstaff, AZ (Fall 20___)
- Wrote and implemented Individual Education Plans (IEPs) for nine students. Executed and recorded IEP goals. Developed and implemented creative lesson plans. Eight of nine students showed marked improvement in language arts and math scores at end of year.
- Co-taught in the Multidisciplinary Learning Project. Fourth grade students achieved a 91% passing rate and were eligible to graduate to fifth grade.
- Created and taught FOSS science lessons. Subsequently developed new FOSS-appropriate lessons for "Treetop Ecosystems" and "Wetland Amphibians." End-of-term exams indicated an overall improvement in science scores of 14-31%.
- Selected for Curriculum Coordination Committee by school principal (Mr. Danielson). Devoted more than 50 hours to a reconceptualization of the Social Studies program.
- Worked with two autistic students. Applied observational techniques, developed and taught lessons, and supervised field trips.
- Designed an interactive workshop to introduce teachers to Nearpod and how it can be used to facilitate both science and social studies instruction.

RELATED EXPERIENCE: Innovative Teacher Project Award (Fall 20___)
- Wrote an extensive grant application that won funding for a teacher-developed unit on increasing inquiry-based learning throughout the elementary curriculum.

Camp Naturemore, Sedona, AZ (Summer 20___)
- Selected as a counselor at a summer camp for physically disabled youngsters. Developed programs, taught outdoor lessons, and instructed archery and horseback riding classes. Was asked to return for five consecutive summers.

Third Grade Teacher - Field Experience Semester - South Rim Elementary School, Tusayan, AZ (Spring 20___)
- Teamed with Chapter I reading specialist to assess and teach 34 below level readers. Overall reading achievement scores increased by 22%.

QUOTE: "Connie receives my highest recommendation as a teacher candidate of superior talents and exceptional abilities. Not only will her future students reap the benefits of her engaging curriculum and winning personality; colleagues will also be valued recipients of her leadership, direction, and drive. There is absolutely no question that she will be the ideal teacher. It is my considered opinion that Connie's talents, skills and attitude place her in the top tier of all the new teachers entering the profession."
- Mr. Bradley Danielson, Principal - Ponderosa Elementary

This resume stands out as being very easy to read (the applicant has placed all her information in visually-acceptable blocks of text) in addition to including a defining quote at the end. The fact that the quote comes from a fellow administrator puts a professional exclamation point on this very strong resume.

Jasmine Rice

8900 E. Broadway
Burlington, VT 05405

Cell: 802-555-2323
jasminer@xxx.net

Objective:
Sixth Grade Science Teacher

Qualifications:
- Dedicated and enthusiastic teacher with extensive experience in science education.
- Skilled in adapting to individual student strengths and weaknesses; innate ability to adapt instruction for specific needs.
- Talented classroom manager with a clear focus on time-on-task and purposeful use of instructional time.
- Clear focus on the value of inquiry-based science instruction and the roles played by both teacher and students.
- Positive, engaging personality who values clear and constant communication as a springboard to effective instruction.
- Thoroughly enjoys and relishes cooperative teaching/learning strategies that promote science as an everyday operation.

"Jasmine's knowledge of subject matter is exceeded only by the creative and dynamic ways she is able to share her knowledge with others." - Dr. Andrew Logan, Principal, White Mountain Middle School

Education and Certification:
- University of Vermont, Burlington, VT • Bachelor of Science in Education, Fall 20__
- GPA: 3.91/4.00.
- Elementary Education (K-6) - Level I

Professional Experience:
- Taught sixth grade science during student teaching. Was given full responsibility for entire class during the fourth week and carried out all instructional responsibilities in a systematic and purposeful environment.
- Assessed 24 students via the Academic Assessment Consortium. Results indicate that students showed significant progress and improvement (32%) on the State Science Exams given at the end of the term.
- Presented a "Science Through Children's Literature" workshop at the Vermont Science Teachers Association in October 20__.
- Directed and coordinated the "Everyday Science" grant at the invitation of the school principal. Was awarded a letter of commendation for efforts in raising attitudes towards science by substantial amounts.
- Designed an entire sixth grade Envirothon for 211 students. Teacher feedback was extremely positive and complimentary.
- Mentored three ESL students in an after-school science program ("Backyard Science") designed to offer hands-on opportunities for below-level pupils.
- Developed curricula, assembled teaching materials, prepared goals and agendas, created lesson plans, and taught five sections of General Science.

"Jasmine has a marvelous ability to 'take charge' and develop an engaging partnership with others - fostering a team approach to learning and discovery." - Ms. Samantha Wilcox, Cooperating Teacher, White Mountain Middle School.

Professional Profile:
- Recipient of the Outstanding Student Teacher Award from the University of Vermont Department of Education, November 20__.
- Vice-president, Student Education Association, University of Vermont, 20__ to 20__.
- Member, Vermont State Science Teachers Association, 20__ to 20__.
- Co-presenter (with Dr. Adam Mancuso), National Science Teacher Association, April 20__ ("Making Inquiry-based Science Work for Beginning Teachers.").
- Fluent in Spanish, Portuguese, and Italian.
- Volunteer tutor, Burlington Literacy Council

"Jasmine's dedication to excellence produced stimulating student projects, energizing lessons, and magnificent instructional units across the entire science curriculum." - Mr. William McFarland, White Mountain Science Supervisor.

> Here's another resume that effectively uses reviews and quotes from professional educators to highlight her skills and talents. Those quotes have been systematically placed in strategic locations to give additional emphasis to her qualifications. The addition of a Professional Profile also adds considerable weight to this document.

Part II

Writing an A+ Cover Letter

Chapter 15

__What Nobody Told You About Cover Letters__

Have you ever been on a blind date? Your roommate or best friend tells you about this really awesome guy who's good looking (naturally), has a terrific personality (of course), is a forward on the college's soccer team, has sparkling eyes, a great sense of humor, and is a fantastic dancer. You agree to go out with him, anticipating a night full of wonderful conversations, interesting parties, and, who knows, maybe even a little romance.

However, when the guy shows up it's very clear that he is either the son of Frankenstein or some alien mutation from another planet. He can barely speak, is exceedingly nervous, and has two left feet. He's socially awkward and has no clue on how to carry a conversation. The night drags and you can hardly wait to get back to your dorm and slam your roommate for setting you up with the weirdest guy on campus. What a waste!

Well, guess what? Cover letters and blind dates are often similar. For example, you only got a minimal amount of information about the blind date from your roommate. She just gave you some basic, though very incomplete, data. She wanted to hook you up with this guy, so she only told you the good stuff (at least the "good stuff" according to her). There were some essential details she left out – either intentionally or unintentionally – things you quickly discovered on your own.

The same holds true for cover letters. You may have only a modicum of information about these documents – information you've been able to troll from your friends or professors. Some of that information may be true and some may be false…and some may be completely incomprehensible. And, it is highly likely that, like a blind date, there's some information that is clearly missing – critical information you need ahead of time in order to craft a dynamic and purposeful cover letter, one that will get the attention of a busy school administrator looking for a new faculty member.

I'd like to share some important stuff you really need to know about cover letters. On the other hand (and unfortunately) I don't have any important stuff to share about your next blind date. Sorry!

Your cover letter is not #1. I'd like you to do something unusual: Stop reading this book! Not to worry, we'll be back shortly. Now, close the book and look at the cover – specifically the title. You will notice that the main title (*Ace Your Teacher Resume*) is in large bold letters (about 72-point font). Look again and you will see that the second part of the title (*and Cover Letter*) is in a considerably smaller font size (about 24-point font). In short, the main part of the title was printed in considerably larger type than the secondary part of the book's title. There was a very good reason for that.

It's because your cover letter is less important than your resume.

You may have received some advice from well-meaning people that your cover letter is a critical part of your teacher application process…and it is. BUT (and this is a big BUT), it is not as important as your resume. I know that sounds counter-intuitive simply because the cover letter is the first item in the collection of papers that makes up your application to a school or district. The next item in that stack of papers is, quite often, the resume. So, logically, you would assume that the most important piece of paper goes on top, the next most important piece goes next, the third most important piece…and so on.

Wrong!

Here's the reality. A significant majority of principals and school district administrators will look at the resume first, then they will look at the cover letter. You'll place the cover letter on the top of your application pile, but it will be the resume that will often be the first document read. Your resume will get the initial screening (remember six seconds?). If it "passes" that initial screening, then it will be read in its entirety. If it succeeds in that more complete screening, then the cover letter will be read in order to confirm and verify the information in the resume and determine whether the entire application packet goes into the "YES" pile or the "NO" pile.

INSIDER TIP

A well-crafted and well-written cover letter is designed to highlight your competencies, skills, achievements, and qualifications (listed in the resume) as they relate specifically to the posted position. As a result, the critical question you need to answer in a cover letter is: "In what ways do my qualifications and experiences address the specific needs of this school or district."

Your cover letter is a narrative summary of your resume. Your cover letter adds personality to your resume. It is not a "stand alone" document; rather it is intended to confirm the first impression engendered by the resume. When a principal scans or reviews your resume she or he will form an initial impression about you ("She has a wide variety of experiences with children far beyond her course requirements and student teaching semester." "He has a lot of ambition and drive – devoting a lot of time working with other teachers to establish various after school programs for academically challenged students."). After formulating that first impression, a reader will want some type of confirmation; some validation that the initial thoughts about a candidate are accurate and precise. That's one of the chief functions of the cover letter.

FROM THE PRINCIPAL'S DESK:

"A good cover letter is one that personalizes the candidate and explains why they would be a great choice for the position."

A cover letter won't get you an interview. A good cover letter will, however, verify that you are a highly qualified individual who meets the specifications of the job. The initial judgement about you is established by the resume; the cover letter corroborates that verdict. As I hope you've gathered from the discussion above, a cover letter is written to enhance your resume as well as highlight other information which may not be a part of your resume. In essence, a cover letter should complement the resume, and not repeat phrases or information from the resume.

For example, your resume will state basic facts and information about you (e.g. "Established an after-school inventor's club for grades 3-5 at Pinedale Elementary School which focused on higher-level thinking strategies – resulting in a 19% improvement in Overall Scores on the California Critical Thinking Skills Tests."). Your cover letter is where you can then place that accomplishment in the context of the school's needs (e.g. "As indicated on the Columbia River School District's web site 'improvement in critical thinking abilities' is a priority goal for every school. During my student teaching semester I developed and administered a program focused on improving students' cognitive processing skills. I would enthusiastically welcome the opportunity to bring my talents, desire and ambition to make that a successful reality at Wild Salmon Elementary School."

Remember: The resume states, the cover letter confirms.

A TOUCH OF HUMOR

Here's a candidate I'm sure any school would be thrilled to have:

"Special Skills: I've got a Ph.D. in human feelings."

Good cover letters are not mass produced. Following are the opening paragraphs of two separate cover letters. For the moment, imagine you are a high school principal with a position to fill. Based entirely on these two examples, which person would you be most inclined to interview?

A.

To Whom It May Concern:

I recently came across your job posting for a 10th grade Biology teacher. I think my skills and experience would be a good match for the position and I am submitting my resume to you in hopes of obtaining an interview.

B.

Dear Mr. Blocker:

Superior High School's web site states "Excellence in teaching; success in learning" as their operational motto. I believe my experiences as a soon to be certified Biology teacher can help promote that maxim to all your students as you begin the forthcoming revision of the Biology curriculum. I would welcome both the opportunity and challenge of working with other teachers to design a Biology program clearly focused on outstanding instruction and high academic standards.

I would imagine you selected person "B" as the one you would be most inclined to meet (and interview). Why? Simply because she or he wrote a cover letter that was tailored specifically for you...a letter that was clearly directed at your specific needs. The obvious problem with the "A" letter is that it is generic and could be used to apply for any job in any school in any district in any state. In other words, it's a "one size fits all" letter. There's a good chance that the person who wrote it is running off multiple copies and sending it out to every school in the universe with a job opening.

Despite what you may have heard, cover letters are not mass publications. Each one must be unique, singular, and targeted to a specific school, a specific district, and/or a specific teaching position. Do not (and I repeat) **do not** make the fatal mistake of writing a generic cover letter. It will be spotted in an instant and it will surely take a brief journey directly into the nearest trash can. Form (cover) letters will certainly kill any chance you have of ever getting a job.

FROM THE PRINCIPAL'S DESK:

"Is the cover letter a standard letter sent to 30 other schools, or is it specific to my school and my needs, clearly linked to the candidate's strengths?"

Good cover letters are not templates. For a moment, imagine that today is your birthday. You go out to your mailbox and find the following letter:

Dear: ❏ Son, ❏ Daughter, ❏ Nephew, ❏ Niece, ❏ Friend, ☑ Student:

I would like to wish you a very happy: ☑ birthday, ❏ anniversary, ❏ bar mitzvah, ❏ Halloween.

Today is a very special: ☑ celebration, ❏ honor, ❏ pastime, ❏ day – one you will always: ❏ remember, ☑ cherish, ❏ laugh at, ❏ fall asleep at.

It is also an important: ❏ moment, ☑ year, ❏ ceremony, ❏ joke in your life and that means it is a time to ☑ party, ❏ go back to sleep, ❏ write a term paper, ❏ do some base jumping.

Here's to a very: ❏ happy, ❏ confusing, ☑ unbelievable, ❏ contemplative day!

Sincerely,

❏ Your Favorite Aunt, ❏ Loving Mother, ❏ Grandma Betty, ☑ The author of a book on resumes (and cover letters)

There are a number of web sites where you can download templates for cover letters, fill in the blanks, print them out, and send them off to dozens, if not hundreds, of potential employers. Perhaps your college's career center has a number of cover letter templates you can use to draft your own cover letter in an effort to save time.

I have one very clear word of advice about using cover letter templates: **DON'T**.

While you will undoubtedly save a lot of time by using previously-prepared templates, you will also be setting yourself up for a great deal of failure. No template in the world can showcase the real you – only you can do that. A cover letter, above all else, is your chance to "marry" your personality and your potential contributions to a school/district with the skills and talents enumerated on your resume. No template can ever make that connection.

Also, keep in mind that administrators can spot a template a mile away. After having read hundreds, thousands, or even hundreds of thousands of cover letters over the years it is quite easy to pick out the impersonal template from the more personal cover letters. And, if you and a couple of hundred of your classmates all use the same cover letter templates (from your college), then you are just making a busy school administrator's job that much easier. Everybody's letter will look so similar and so familiar that it will be quite easy to put them all in the same category: the "**NO**" category!

A TOUCH OF HUMOR

This was included in one (very confused) applicant's cover letter:

"I believe that weakness is the first level of strength, given the right attitude and driving force. My school advised me to fix my punctuality...."

I like to think of a cover letters as an opportunity for you to reach out to a principal or school district administrator as a highly qualified individual, not just as an applicant. In other words, the resume outlines your skills and experiences; the cover letter gives those skills and experiences personality. Or, let's go back to the blind date you had at the beginning of this chapter. The resume is your friend telling you about all the attributes of a person you are about to go out with. The cover letter is the actual date – where you truly learn about the individual's personality and how those attributes actually match up with the real person.

Here's to lots of great dates!

Chapter 16

Insider Secret:
How to Stand Out Over the Competition

In a previous book – *Ace Your Teacher Interview: 149 Fantastic Answers to Tough Interview Questions, 2nd Ed.* (Indianapolis, IN: Blue River Press, 2016) – I devoted an entire section (Chapter 6) to the single-most important question teacher candidates must always answer in an interview. Here's the first part of that chapter:

> *It's the one question that is always in the mind of any interviewer. It doesn't matter whether you are interviewing for a job stocking shelves at a local grocery store, interviewing for the CEO position at a major company, or interviewing for a position as the manager of a minor league baseball club – every interviewer has this question on her or his mind when they interview candidates for a position. And here's why it is important – the question will never be asked in any interview...but it must always be answered.*
>
> *The question is this:*
>
> How will this person make my job easier?
>
> *You are being interviewed because the interviewer hopes you can bring value, dedication, and expertise to the job. Those qualities are what any boss wants to see in her or his employees. Those qualities help the boss (principal) do her or his job better and ensure that a product (education) gets into the hands of the consumer (students). That single question will never come up in any teacher interview (or any other kind of interview for that matter), but if you can answer the question – several times during the interview – you will put yourself heads and shoulders above the rest of the competition and ensure a very favorable assessment on the interview.*
>
> How will this person make my job easier?

The significance of that all-important question is threefold:

1. Any principal wants teachers who are solely focused on the instructional needs of students. If all you want is a job or long summer vacations, then you are not satisfying what the principal wants or needs for her or his school. In other words, if you are in it for yourself, then you're obviously not in it for kids.

2. Administrators are looking for people who can solve problems, not create problems. If you can demonstrate ways in which you can contribute to the effective and efficient running of a school (rather that to the headaches of a principal) you will be a positive addition to any school faculty.

3. Teaching is challenging. If you are one who has the skills and talents to meet those challenges – head on – then you will be one the principal can count on to address those issues, rather than having to take the responsibility herself or himself to do it for you. The bottom line is this: Are you responsible and are you willing to shoulder the everyday responsibilities of a professional educator?

Your ability to answer that critical question in an interview is essential to your success in landing a teaching position. But, it is equally important in a cover letter for the simple reason that the cover letter (and accompanying resume) might be how you get the interview in the first place. That is, your cover letter must be written in such a way as to let a principal (a potential employer) know that you are focused more on the school's needs than on your own personal needs. More than 90% of your competition will ignore that critical principle. You should not.

Let's take a look at the first part of an applicant's cover letter and see if he has answered the question above:

Bruce Springstream
123 Grammy Ave.
Asbury Park, NJ 07712

Mr. Chip Munk, Principal
Furry Creature Elementary School
987 Mammal Lane
Big Bear, CA 92315

Hello Mr. Munk:

My name is Bruce Springstream and I'd like to apply for the third grade teacher position at your school. I'm really a good teacher because my cooperating teacher in student teaching gave me high marks. I really like to work with kids and I think I can do a very good job teaching the students at your school. I have lots of teachers in my family including my mother and a sister, so teaching is sort of "in my blood." I guess I was just born to be a teacher.

As you'll see by my resume I have done lots of stuff. I have a lot of experiences working with kids in summer camp and at the local YMCA.

So, what do you think? It should be obvious that here is an individual who has no intention of ever answering the critical question posed at the start of this chapter. Here is an individual who is more interested in promoting himself than he is in addressing the specific needs of a principal or school. He has done absolutely nothing to answer the critical question in the mind of the reader. In short, this is a letter about him, not about answering the #1 question in an administrator's mind.

A TOUCH OF HUMOR

One job applicant for a teaching position shared the following experience:

"Child care provider: Organized activities; prepared lunches and snakes."

Here's one of the cruel realities of teacher recruitment: A principal is NOT interested in hiring you (ouch!). She or he is interested in hiring the most qualified person for the job. If that happens to be you, then fine. If it happens to be someone else, then that is fine (by the principal), too. In other words **YOU** are not the commodity…the **BEST QUALIFIED PERSON** is the commodity the principal wants to bring into her or his school.

As a result, when writing a cover letter, it is critically important to keep the focus off you. For example, if your cover letter sounds the least bit self-serving, egocentric, narcissistic or carries a "here I am" tone (like the example in the box above), it will surely violate the principle in the paragraph above. And, it will, most definitely, ensure your letter a short one-way trip to the trash can.

INSIDER TIP

You can soar above your competition by writing a cover letter that demonstrates the <u>value you will bring to the school</u>, rather than a cover letter about you. Always keep a principal's needs in mind when drafting your letter. You can do that by demonstrating one or more of the following:
- How you can solve problems
- How you can deliver benefits to students or the school
- How you are willing to go "above and beyond" the usual teacher duties
- How you have always put students first
- How you bring added value to the school
- How you are willing to "go the extra mile"
- How you put the employer's needs above your own needs

Look at the bulleted items (in the box above) again. You should notice a consistent theme in each of those items. The emphasis, in each case, is on the employer's needs and not necessarily on your desire for some gainful employment. The emphasis should not be on "I want a job!", but rather on "What can I do for you." If, for example, you can show how you can solve problems or how you are willing to go beyond your assigned duties, then you will have effectively answered that very critical question.

FROM THE PRINCIPAL'S DESK:

"The cover letter should express interest in the position/district. It should also highlight how the candidate would be able to support the mission of the school district because of their experiences."

Let's take a look at the beginning of another applicant's cover letter to see how she effectively answers "How will this person make my job easier?"

Misty Morning
987 State St., Apt. 111
Denver, CO 80210

April 12, 20__

Dr. Noah Lott, Principal
Mount Sopris Elementary School
351 Main St.
Carbondale, CO 81623

Dear Dr. Lott:

If you are looking for a hard-working, committed, and "never-give-up" educator, then I'd like to be your next third grade teacher.

As a pre-service teacher with extensive experiences in working with educationally-challenged youngsters, I believe I have quite a lot to offer your students. I bring more than 10 years of work with children as a camp counselor, Sunday School teacher, teacher's aide, nature center volunteer, and student teacher in concert with a keen eagerness to ensure both the cognitive and affective growth of each and every student. I particularly enjoy working as a contributing member of a dedicated team of teachers focused on innovative and results-oriented educational initiatives – particularly for special needs children.

Some of my key experiences relevant to Mount Sopris Elementary School include:

- My volunteer work with the Sierra Club in leading backpacking trips through Rocky Mountain National Park could be used to further the school's Outdoor Education Initiative.

- With a minor in Spanish I would relish the opportunity to contribute to the ELL program through a concentrated series of in-school and after-school projects.

- Having developed several parent workshops focused on the Common Core, I would embrace the opportunity to foster increased family involvement through your School Accountability Committee (SAC).

Can you see the difference? What becomes very clear with the sample cover letter in the box above is that here is an individual who is more interested in contributing to a specific school than she is in satisfying her own personal needs. The tone of her letter and her careful attention to its wording underscores her commitment to teaching and the ways in which she might effectively address the educational demands of a specific school. It is less about her and more about what she can do for the school.

Short story: She is answering the critical question. And, so can you…in your cover letter!

A TOUCH OF HUMOR

I don't know about you, but I just don't think this is something I would want to feature in a cover letter (apparently someone did):

"Favorite Activities: Playing trivia games. I am a repository of worthless knowledge."

Chapter 17

<u>More Strategies for Success</u>

Your cover letter has two jobs: first, it shines a spotlight on your resume. And second, it adds a voice and personality to your basic credentials – a personality that's pleasant and interesting enough to be invited in for a face-to-face meeting.

Below are some tips and tricks that will distinguish your cover letter and help it stand out (in a positive way) from the competition. Always keep these in mind as you draft this all-important document.

1. <u>NEVER</u> (notice the capital letters and bold type) send a cover letter that is more than one page in length. First of all, most principals just don't have the time necessary to read expansive and extensive cover letters. Second, if you are just starting down the road of your teaching career you just don't have enough experiences to create a letter that would require more than one page. And, third, if you were to submit a two or three page cover letter the first impression any reader would get is that you were "padding" your qualifications or that you were trying to hide something from your past with a barrage of flashy vocabulary, longwinded sentences, and elongated paragraphs.

You will be doing any administrator a great favor by keeping the cover letter to a single page.

FROM THE PRINCIPAL'S DESK:

"[For a cover letter] less is often more. Be clear and precise with your information. You do not need to shrink your font to "8" and try to fill an entire page. It's simply more opportunity to create unwanted errors. We simply want to get to know a little about you and your desire to become a teacher. We'll learn more about you in the interview."

2. Three Paragraphs. As you will learn in Chapter 18, there are three basic parts (three basic paragraphs) of a good cover letter. These include the following:

- Opening Paragraph. This paragraph is designed to confirm who you are, your reason for writing, and the message you wish to communicate to the reader.

- The Body. This is where the "selling" takes place. It is your opportunity to demonstrate how your unique talents and experiences can contribute to the overall welfare of a school or district.

- The Closing. This is your opportunity to make a (good) final impression. This paragraph will ultimately determine whether the reader puts you in the "YES" pile or calls you in for an interview.

Bottom line – three paragraphs (period).

INSIDER TIP

You can increase the readability (the ease of reading) of your cover letter by increasing the line spacing. I suggest a 120% increase over your selected font size (typically 12-point). To do this in Word 2013, block your entire cover letter using the left button on your mouse (or click on Select on the far right end of the toolbar and then click Select All). Click on the "Home" tab, and then click on the small arrow in the lower right corner of Paragraph. Then, in the Line Spacing pulldown select Exactly and set the spacing to two points above the size of your font (14-point if you're using a 12-point font). This will automatically expand the line spacing throughout the document and make it less crowded and more readable. Make sure, however, that this doesn't expand your cover letter to more than one page. If it does, then you might need to do some editing or revising.

3. Spelling and Grammar Count. As you have most likely gathered from earlier chapters in this book, spelling and grammar do count...a great deal. In my conversations with principals from around the country it became very clear that spelling and grammatical errors were the primary criterion that eliminated most potential candidates from any further review. One principal told me she recently advertised for a position in her school. When all was said and done, she had received 192 applications for that single position. She said the first part of her job was easy, simply because she knew from prior experience that many of those applicants made the fatal mistake of sending documents that had both spelling and grammatical mistakes. In less than an hour she was able to eliminate 157 applications from the pool for one distinctive reason – all of them misspelled words or used improper grammar. If you're doing the math, that means that more than 81 percent of all the applications were eliminated within the first few seconds of opening them.

What is sad is that there may have been a truly outstanding teacher in that pile of discarded applications – a teacher that would have truly made a difference in the lives of students, someone who would have made unique and positive contributions to the school's academic programs, and an educator who would have answered the critical question posed in the beginning of the preceding chapter. But, they were eliminated because they didn't take the time to proofread their cover letter.

It should come as no surprise that one of the critical skills for every teacher is the ability to communicate effectively. You need to communicate with your students, their parents, the administration of the school, and with the general public. If you can't demonstrate good communication skills via your cover letter, then the reader of that letter knows that communication in the other aspects of teaching may be a challenge for you. In other words, your ability to communicate effectively and accurately via a cover letter is your first "test" of whether you have what it takes to be an accomplished educator. Fail this one test and you are, quite simply, out!

FROM THE PRINCIPAL'S DESK:

"The most common mistake teacher candidates make on their cover letters are grammatical or simple typos. It appears, or is the perception, that the applicant rushes to complete something without paying attention to little details. Triple check and then check again before having another person or two check the document."

4. Write to a Real Person. If you send your cover letter to "Dear Sirs" or 'To Whom It May Concern" you will be demonstrating to a potential employer that you are so lazy and insufficiently concerned to discover the name of the person in charge of hiring. You are also sending another dangerous signal – that is, you are taking the easy way out by generating a slew of all-purpose cover letters (with identical salutations) and disseminating them across a broad range of districts and schools. Bad idea!

Find out the name of the person in charge…a real human being! Address your letter to an actual person, not a title. This is a critical homework assignment and there are no shortcuts. Don't cop out on this one for the sake of efficiency. Do whatever is necessary to discover someone's name and position. Trust me, it will make a difference!

FROM THE PRINCIPAL'S DESK:

"A candidate's cover letter is most impressive when it is addressed to the correct individual and the name of the individual is spelled correctly."

5. Rewrite for Each Individual School/District. If you are like the hundreds of future graduates who visit your college's career development center (or some similar career guidance office on campus) each semester, you will, most likely, get a packet of material on how to write successful resumes and cover letters. And, just like all those other people visiting the career center you will also receive a sample or two of a good cover letter to be included in your application materials. And, just like everyone else, you will draft a single cover letter (based on your college's sample letter) that you will use as part of every job application you submit. You may change the name and address on every cover letter you submit, but essentially the cover letter will have the same format, same content, and same information no matter to whom it is sent.

I have one word for that process: **DON'T!**

Sending the same cover letter to every school you apply to can be the proverbial "kiss of death!" If you sound just like everyone else applying for the job, then there will be nothing to distinguish you from the masses; there will be nothing to identify you as a singularly unique and distinctive teacher who can bring added value to the students in a particular school. Once again, you will look like one of many, rather than one of a kind.

FROM THE PRINCIPAL'S DESK:

"With information available on the web, and the District's own site, a cover letter should be stacked with how you can contribute to the district and specific programs within the district. Budget, initiatives, vision, all of that. Your cover letter should be tailored to each district."

What I'm going to suggest instead is that you tailor each cover letter to the specific demands and needs of a particular school. Will that mean more work for you – ABSOLUTELY! Instead of spending your time crafting one all-purpose letter to be sent to all the job openings, you will need to craft individual letters – a different one for each and every job posting. You need to craft a cover letter that is tied directly to the needs and wants of a specific school, not to the generalities of the entire education marketplace. In doing so, you will be sending a most refreshing message to the reader of a cover letter – "This person took the time to read my job posting and tailor her or his message to my specific needs. This is a person who puts my desires (a quality education program) ahead of her or his desires (getting a job). This is a person I want to bring in for an interview."

Cover letters written in direct response to the actual needs of a school are what I like to call "Respect Letters" because they demonstrate a respect for the administrator and the school by indicating a direct match between what the job posting asks for and what the candidate can deliver in direct response to that posting. In many cases, those letters will use words and terms from the posting in order to showcase how the applicant can meet those needs. Jeffrey Fox, author of *Don't Send a Resume*, advises letter writers to: "Flatter the person who wrote the ad with your response letter. Echo the author's words and intent. Your letter should be a mirror of the ad." Fox notes that when the recipient reads such a letter, the thought process will be: "This person seems to fit the description. This person gets it."[1]

One of the ways in which you can be sure to tailor each cover letter to the specifics of a single job posting is to design a "T-square" – a two-column structure that allows you to begin matching the needs of the school with your own personal list of skills, talents, and expertise. The left-hand column is used to list the specific needs of the school as listed in the job posting. The right-hand column is for your attributes and skills that meet each of those specific needs. Here's what a blank T-square looks like:

Job Posting	Matching Skills

To demonstrate how a T-square might be used let's create a fictitious example. In this case, the principal at Frog Creek Middle School (Mr. Tad Pohl) posts the following position on a job search web site for teachers:

---

1   Fox, Jeffrey. *Don't Send a Resume: And Other Contrarian Rules to Help Land a Great Job.* (New York: Hachette Books, 2001).

Position Summary: Frog Creek Middle School is seeking an English teacher. Preferred candidates will have considerable experiences in working with middle-level students. In addition, the candidate will have a proven record of contributions to the life of a school in co-curricular areas beyond the classroom, especially coaching and advising students.

Essential Duties and Responsibilities

- Teach multiple sections
- Prepare course materials such as syllabi, homework assignments, and handouts in print and in our online course management system
- Maintain student attendance records, grades, and other required records
- Design, evaluate, and grade students' class work, assignments, papers, and examinations
- Plan, evaluate, and revise curricula, course content, course materials, and methods of instruction
- Maintain regularly scheduled office hours in order to advise and assist students
- Participate in the school evaluation and professional development programs
- Advise students on academic and other matters in accordance with the School's mission
- Coach an athletic team and/or advise an extracurricular activity as required
- Participate in some infrequent evening or weekend activities, including meetings, professional development, or other school activities
- Other duties, as assigned

Posted: March 12, 20__

Starting Date: August 22, 20__

Carrie O'Donnell was in her student teaching semester at Slippery Slope State College. Placed with a veteran middle school teacher, she was excited about getting a middle school teaching position in a local middle school. As soon as she saw the posting (above) she began to put together a T-square in preparation for writing her application cover letter. Here is part of her first draft:

Job Posting	Matching Skills
• Plan, evaluate, and revise curricula, course content, course materials	• Developed a three-week thematic unit on "American Masters"
• Design, evaluate, and grade students' class work	• Maintained records for 112 students during student teaching
• Coach an athletic team	• Co-coached the junior varsity softball team
• Participate in some infrequent evening or weekend activities	• Established a 'Homework Council" involving parents

In her cover letter Carrie wrote: "During my student teaching semester I planned, evaluated and revised curricula with a self-initiated three-week thematic unit on 'American Literature Masters.' I can bring that same level of dedication and creativity to Frog Creek Middle School."

As you can see, the T-square design assisted Carrie in designing a cover letter that was in line with the specific job responsibilities posted online. As a result, she was able to draft a cover letter that spoke directly to the principal – a letter that indicated that her qualifications were in line with the specific needs of the school. Rather than submit an all-purpose letter ("I am a highly qualified individual who would like to contribute my skills to your school") – a letter that could be used for every job posting – Carrie was able to design a cover letter that addressed the specifics of a single posting. She made sure she was the one candidate with the skills and talents the school was looking for. Bottom line: she talked about specifics, rather than generalities.

6. Sell Your Achievements. You want to separate yourself from the pack (stand out from the "herd," so to speak). Because so many other applicants will look more alike than different, it is essential that you differentiate yourself from everyone else. Your intent in a cover letter is not to answer a question such as, "Who are you?" Rather, the letter should focus on a more critical query, "What can you do for me?" Cover letters that simply list all the stuff you did during your student teaching semester are dull, dry, and commonplace. They all sound the same (making you one of the herd). Instead, you want to answer the more critical question ("What can you, specifically, do for me?") – satisfying the needs of an administrator, rather than merely listing common responsibilities and tasks of all the other applicants.

Think how you have benefitted the schools, youth organizations, summer camps, and other child-related organizations (both formal and informal) where you have worked or volunteered. You might want to consider how you helped those organizations by:

- Increasing student achievement (higher test scores, better mid-term or final grades, improved grades on homework)

- Improving existing programs (revising a curriculum, modifying a series of lessons, rewriting textual materials)

- Positively enhancing attitudes (improved levels of attendance, more active classroom performance, more engaged students)

- Enhancing levels of faculty morale (contests, special celebrations, recognition ceremonies)

- Creating new and innovative programs/projects (new teaching units, creative in-service seminars, engaging after-school academic projects)

- Winning awards, honors, and commendations (distinguished academic achievement, improved test scores, school board recognition)

As you consider your achievements, also consider two key ingredients that you definitely want to share with a reader: 1) What was it you specifically did, and 2) how did it benefit the school or organization. Most cover letters focus almost exclusively on the first ingredient and forget the second one. It is the <u>benefits you have implemented</u> that will make your cover letter shine above all the others.

It is essential that you clearly define what you have to offer a school in relationship to its specific needs AND the results that might ensue if they were to bring you on board. In mathematical terms it would be the following formula: Contribution + Results = "Wow, we really want to hire this person for our school!"

INSIDER TIP

Most cover letters mistakenly focus on either a narrative regurgitation of information presented in the resume or an additional listing of what the applicant has done in his/her life or with students. Distinguish yourself by having two to three different responses (woven throughout the cover letter) to the pressing question of all administrators, "How will this person make my job easier?"

Here are a few examples:

- "Positive reviews from Dr. Sutherland, my college supervisor, indicate that 'I overflow with historical curiosity.' I would like to share that passion with students at Fairfield High School as you complete and implement the new American History curriculum."

- "As the Assistant Director of Camp Wildcat I effectively managed all the sports programs for more than 120 youngsters. I believe my organizational skills and attention to detail would be positive assets as a physical education teacher at Cloverdale Elementary School."

- "I am an extremely high-energy and enthusiastic teacher! During my student teaching placement in Miss Hawkins 9th grade algebra class students exhibited significantly improved attitudes on the Student Attitude Survey (S.A.S.) at the end of the year."

FROM THE PRINCIPAL'S DESK:

"Be specific, do your homework, and then write with voice and style. I assess the candidate's ability to write when reading this letter."

Here's a key word that will ensure the success of any cover letter: **Match**. That is, your cover letter must indicate in several ways, a match between your qualifications and skills and the specific needs of the school or district. Writing a generic or "form" letter will not accomplish this. Using the same identical letter for each and every school opening will not do this either. To stand out you must do what most everyone else won't – write a cover letter that is specific, detailed, and precise… oh, one more, a letter that is specifically tailored for only one school and/ or district.

Yes, this will mean more homework for you. You'll have to scour each school's web page for pertinent information, you'll have to check out any brochures, pamphlets or newsletters disseminated by each school/ district, and you may have to interview various individuals in a community for their thoughts and perceptions. You may want to visit a school and/or district to view several classrooms or talk with various teachers. In short, just to write a single cover letter, you may have to do lots of extra work (rather than duplicating the sample cover letters provided a career center…or this book). And then you'll have to do it all over again for the next cover letter…and the next…and the next. But, guess what, you'll be the only one who does that and the only one who gets multiple invitations to interview with several schools. The result may be multiple job offers. Now, won't all that work be worth it?

Chapter 18

<u>Anatomy of a Sensational Cover Letter</u>

Here's an event that may bring back some memories (pleasant or otherwise). I distinctly remember a Biology lesson I experienced in my sophomore year in high school. It was when Mr. Thomas laid out several flat trays throughout the lab. He then gave each team a single earthworm along with several metal tools and took us step-by-step through an extended dissection of that poor unfortunate invertebrate. My partner and I carefully slit our worm from its clitellum up to its head with a very sharp scalpel. With a teasing needle we carefully and slowly spread the skin of our worm. We then inserted some pins to hold the skin down. Using the needle and a pair of tweezers we gently removed the various organs to a separate part of the tray. Consulting a chart in the front of the lab we attempted to identify most of the parts before us. We then proceeded to color in an elaborate illustration of a common earthworm Mr. Thomas had provided for us. The dissection was slow and deliberate and there were, as you might imagine, many comments about "cruel and unusual punishment" as well as the usual repertoire of sophomore humor.

Then, it was time for lunch.

You, too, might remember dissecting a worm during a Biology class, either in high school or college. Like me, you might remember the names of some of the various parts you removed from your special critter. Organs such as the seminal vesicles, the ventral blood vessel, crop, gizzard, heart, and intestine; and systems such as the circulatory, reproductive, digestive, and nervous system were all laid bare. The concept was that if we understood the various parts that make up a common earthworm we would also understand how the earthworm functions, lives and survives.

So it is that we will now dissect a common cover letter. We will lay bare its various parts so we can begin to understand how it functions and what it should do. I will not, however, require that you use any dissecting tools or engage in the systematic torturing of innocent creatures. You're welcome!

For the most part, a cover letter will consist of eight or nine basic elements. Let's take a look:

1. Header: This is the first part of any cover letter. It consists of your name and explicit contact information. Your contact information should make it easy for anyone to get in touch with you quickly and efficiently. Therefore, anything you list here must be up-to-date and current, including your mailing address(es), email address(es), various phone numbers (cell and residence). It is equally important that the header on your cover letter matches (exactly) the header on your resume. You may elect to center your header at the top of the page or to utilize a split header if listing two different mailing addresses. Let's take a look:

Centered Header

Missy Sippy
123 River Road
Waterway, MS 39120
(601) 888-8888
missysippy@xxxx.com

Split Header

Anita Job

Prior to May 17, 20___ :
987 Lake Blvd.
Marquette, MI 49855
(906) 111-1111 (C)
anitajobnow@xxx.com

After May 17, 20___ :
654 Snowcap Lane
Green Bay, WI 54303
(920) 222-2222 (H)
anitajobnow@xxx.com

As you can see in the second example it is often advisable to list both your current address (at college) along with your home address (after graduation). You never know when an administrator might want to contact you to arrange for an interview. If all you have at the top of your cover letter (and your resume) is your college information, then it may be very difficult for someone to contact you after you have graduated and moved back home.

2. Date: It is always advisable to type the letter and mail the letter on the same day. If you type up a bunch of letters (and date them) on one day and then wait two weeks (for example) to mail them out, it may raise a question in the reader's mind as to the discrepancy between the two events. Type and mail on the same day.

INSIDER TIP

If possible, drop your letter at the post office so it will arrive at its destination on Tuesday. Tuesday is the lightest mail day of the week and your letter will get more attention than if it was to arrive on a Monday (the heaviest mail day). Avoid posting your letters on a Friday or Saturday – that would mean they would, most likely, arrive on a Monday. By the same token, don't post your letters to arrive on a Friday (most administrators want to clear their desks for the weekend). Overall, your letter will get the most attention if it arrives at its destination on a Tuesday (1st choice), Wednesday (2nd choice), or Thursday (3rd choice).

3. Inside Address: This includes the contact name, title, school or district name, street address or P.O. Box number, city, state, and zip code. If you have both a street address and a post office box, list the post office box below the street address (on both the cover letter and envelope). Postal sorting machinery reads from the bottom up and will deliver to the lowest line when given both a street and box number. Make certain that the zip code identifies the box number and not the street address.

If the name of the contact person is not listed with a job posting take time to find out who that person is. Call the school office or the district office and indicate that you are applying for a posted position and would appreciate knowing the name of the person doing the hiring. In addition, make sure you get the correct spelling of that person's name. And (very important) ask for their appropriate title (Mrs., Miss, Ms., Mr., Dr.).

Another option would be to drill down into the district's web site to search for the name of a specific individual. Bottom line: Always use a real person's name (and their official title) for the inside address. It may take extra work on your part, but many candidates don't do this and they essentially "shoot themselves in the foot" as a result.

4. Subject line: This is typically the title of the position for which you are applying. This title also helps connect your cover letter with your resume – since both the subject line and the stated objective on your resume should match. For example, if the listed objective on your resume is "Tenth Grade Social Studies Teacher"; then the subject line on your cover letter should also be "Tenth Grade Social Studies Teacher." The reader then knows that the main text of the cover letter will be focused on a specific job opening. The subject line should be typed flush left.

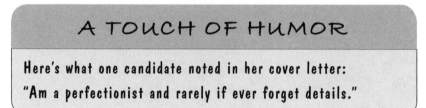

A TOUCH OF HUMOR

Here's what one candidate noted in her cover letter: "Am a perfectionist and rarely if ever forget details."

5. Salutation: The formal word for "Dear so-and-so." This is your initial greeting and, believe me, it carries a lot of weight. It may not seem like a very important part of the cover letter but it has the potential to completely derail any chance you have of getting an interview (or, worse, having the reader toss your letter into the wastebasket). Here are some critical suggestions:

- Addressing your letter to a real person instead of a position or job description will provide a principal or superintendent with a very important piece of information: You're willing to do your homework and get things right!

- When addressing a woman, use either Miss or Mrs. If you are not sure if the individual is married, then you should use the courtesy title Ms.

- If the individual has a doctorate, then use the formal Dr. ("Dear Dr. Smith") in front of the name. Never use Mr., Mrs. Ms. or

Miss. If you're not sure if someone has a doctorate, plan to call the district office and find out.

- Critical: Spell the person's name correctly. Check on this. Double check on this. Spell the person's name incorrectly and you can kiss your chances of a job interview goodbye. For example, look at the cover of this book. You'll notice that my last name is spelled "Fredericks" (note the two e's). If you send me a cover letter and spell my name as 'Fredricks" or "Fredrick" or "Fredicks" I can assure you that your entire application packet will do an inward half-somersault directly into my trash can. That's right, I won't even look at it. Spell my name incorrectly and I'll assume that you didn't take the time to get all your details right. And, if you're not a detail person, you won't be a very good teacher. Short story: Spell it right!

Here is a list of some salutations to use on your cover letter as well as others to avoid:

"Yes" Salutations	"No" Salutations
• Dear Dr. _____	• To Whom It May Concern
• Dear Miss _____	• Dear Sir or Madam
• Dear Mrs. _____	• Dear Personnel Director
• Dear Ms. _____	• Dear Sirs
• Dear Mr. _____	• Dear (School District)
	• Dear (School)
	• Dear Principal
	• Dear Superintendent
	• Hello there

6. Body: This is the main text, or copy, of your cover letter. In most cases it will consist of three paragraphs (which we will discuss in greater detail in the following chapter). Each paragraph will consist of roughly three to six sentences.

- The first paragraph is your introduction. It should be written in an interest-provoking and fascinating manner that clearly separates you from the crowd.

- The second paragraph demonstrates how you are able to address the reader's needs while confirming your skills, talents and abilities.

- The third paragraph should be designed to move the reader towards inviting you for an interview. It is not a summary of your qualifications, but rather an invitation to action.

INSIDER TIP

If you are sending your cover letter via email, you want to keep it as short and sweet as possible. That way, the reader doesn't have to keep scrolling down in order to read the entire letter.

FROM THE PRINCIPAL'S DESK:

"A teacher candidate once told me how excited she would be to work for 'name of school district.' Unfortunately, it was not our school district, the one she was actually applying to, so I put her packet in the NO pile."

7. Complimentary Closing: There are only two closings you should use in your cover letter: "Sincerely" or "Respectfully." Anything else is considered too casual. Salutations such as "Best Regards," "Fondly," "Very Truly Yours," or "All Best Wishes" are considered to be too friendly and, thus, should not be used. If, however, you personally know the individual you are writing to, then it would be O.K. to use one of those closings.

"Yes" Closings	"No" Closings
• Sincerely, • Respectfully,	• Best Regards, • Regards, • Truly Yours, • Very Truly Yours, • Yours Very Truly, • Fondly, • All Best Wishes, • Best Wishes, • Adios, • Ciao, • Later,

8. Writer's Identification: Your writer's identification is your full name – the name you used at the top of the letter as well as the name used at the top of your resume. Make sure all three names are exactly alike. If, for example, your name was "Earl E. Byrd" and that is what you typed at the top of your resume, don't "change' your name to "Earl Edward Byrd" for the top of your cover letter, and then use "Earl Byrd" for your writer's identification. All three instances of your name must be identical. It saves a lot of confusion.

When you sign your name, make sure you sign the same name that is spelled out – never sign with your nickname. For example, if your name is Stanley Cupp, don't sign your letter as "Stan;" sign it as **Stanley Cupp**.

9. Enclosure Notation: Keep in mind that your cover letter is just one part of a larger collection of documents. It is the first piece of paper in that package of materials. Thus, it is always appropriate to type the word *Enclosure* two lines below your name. This gently informs the reader that there is other material to follow. In the unlikely event that your cover letter becomes separated from the rest of your packet, the reader can quickly match them up if this information is provided.

Immediately after the word "Enclosures" indicate the number of additional pieces of information actually included in the envelope. This number reflects the number of separate items, not the total number of all the pages in the application packet. So, if, along with the cover letter, you were to include a resume, a district application form, a copy of your transcript, three letters of recommendation, and a copy of your certification you would use the number (7) after the word "Enclosures." For example: Enclosures (7)

FROM THE PRINCIPAL'S DESK:

"I'm most impressed by a candidate's cover letter when it specifies our district - indicating that the candidate knows or researched us before applying. Something like, 'I have experience with _____ which will benefit the students in the _____ School District.'"

The Complete Anatomy

Your Name
Address
City, State, Zip ← **(Header)**
(999) 999-9999
youremail@xxxx.com

(skip 2 lines)

Date ← **(Date)**

(skip 2 lines)

Contact Person's Name
Title
School or District Name ← **(Inside address)**
Street Address
City, State, Zip

(skip 2 lines)

Re: Title of position applying for ← **(Subject Line)**

(skip 2 lines)

Dear Mr. (Last name of contact person): ← **(Salutation)**

(skip 1 line)

First paragraph of letter begins here. This is the introduction - where
you grab the reader's attention and introduce yourself as a worthy
candidate for the job.

(skip 1 line)

Second paragraph of letter continues here. This is the middle section ← **(Body)**
of your letter that strengthens and supports information from your
resume in a narrative format.

(skip 1 line)

Third paragraph (the closing) of letter goes here. This is the closing
paragraph - the one that summarizes all your qualifications.

(skip 3 lines)

Sincerely, ← **(Complimentary closing)**

(skip 3 lines)

Writer's Identification (your full name - same as at top of letter) ← **(Writer's
Identification)**

(skip 2 lines)

Enclosure ← **(Enclosure notation)**

Chapter 19

<u>Writing a Winner!</u>

Throughout my professional career I've had the honor of writing more than four dozen children's books. Most of the books are nonfiction (e.g. *Around One Rock*; *Desert Night, Desert Day*; *A is for Anaconda*); along with a few fiction titles (e.g. *The Tsunami Quilt: Grandfather's Story*). As a result of those literary efforts, I have been invited, as a visiting author, to scores of schools throughout the United States, Canada, and Mexico. However, there was one visit a few years ago I will never forget.

It was 102° (at 8:00 in the morning) as I walked into the elementary school just outside Las Vegas, NV. I was there to share my books and my literary life with some 700 students. The school's air conditioning was clearly struggling as I began to set up my props in the gymnasium. Soon after morning announcements the students began filing in. Row upon row of students sat on the floor and filled up the gym.

The school librarian introduced me as "the author guy we've been talking about for the past four weeks." I shared a little about myself and began to show slides of my books, talk about the research and writing that went into each one, share elements of the writing process, and describe some forthcoming projects. Fifty-five minutes later, amidst laughter, reams of personal questions ("Is it true your wife is an enchanted princess?") and many anecdotes, the students signaled their appreciation with a thunderous round of applause.

Throughout the remainder of the day, I traveled to various classrooms, sharing some of my books, the writer's life, a couple of valuable writing techniques, and a few of the challenges I face as a children's author. By the end of the day I was tired, but refreshed with the energy of the student body. It was a most satisfying experience – one filled with lots of lessons, lots of inspiration, and lots of magic.

Several weeks later I received a large manila envelope in the mail – the inevitable bundle of thank you letters teachers often ask students to write after an author's visit. Most were the customary "Thank you for coming all the way from Pencil-vania," and "You are my favorite author in the whole world (but don't tell the other authors I said that)," and "I used to have head lice, but now I don't. Can I write a story about that?"

However, on the top of the stack, was one letter neatly printed on blue-lined paper. It immediately caught my eye. I read it over and over and have saved it to this day.

> *Dear Mr. Fredericks,*
>
> *Thank you for coming to read stories to us. It was very interesting and I loved the slugs and the scary story. Well, I got to go. Oh, are you always that sweaty and handsome?*
>
> *Love,*
>
> *Sara Jane*

This is what is known as a winning cover letter!

♦ ♦ ♦

Effective cover letters for teachers are composed of three paragraphs. Each of the three paragraphs has a specific function and a specific job. Let's take a look at each of those paragraphs individually.

First Paragraph

This initial paragraph is your one and only opportunity to capture the reader's attention and entice her or him to read on. Keep in mind you have a very narrow window of opportunity to get that attention so this must be the most polished composition you've ever crafted.

In many respects, your opening paragraph is a sales pitch. As such, it should do two things: tell the reader who you are as well as the specific value you would bring to the school or district. It is not a restatement of the qualities listed on your resume (a focus on you, for example), rather it's an emphatic statement on how your experiences and qualifications will address the specific instructional needs of the school or district. A good opening paragraph will focus on the employer's needs – not you. It is a true "selling" opportunity.

A TOUCH OF HUMOR

In reference to her education, one job applicant stated: "I have a bachelorette degree in computers."

A good opening paragraph starts off with a strong "hook." In the advertising world a "hook" is a phrase or sentence written in such a way that readers are immediately drawn into perusing the rest of an advertisement (and, hopefully, purchasing the product). The "hook" serves to grab the reader's attention – an introduction that is so amazingly interesting, incredibly mysterious, or delightfully thought-provoking that readers just have to keep reading. These first sentences are an inducement to learn more or discover what comes next in the narrative[1].

Often, we are "hooked" into reading a book by its first line(s). It is those first few words that entice us into reading the rest of the story. Here are some famous first lines in literature.

a. Call me Ishmael. – Herman Melville, *Moby-Dick* (1851)

b. It is a truth universally acknowledged, that a single man in possession of a good fortune, must be in want of a wife. – Jane Austen, *Pride and Prejudice* (1813)

c. A screaming comes across the sky. – Thomas Pynchon, *Gravity's Rainbow* (1973)

d. Many years later, as he faced the firing squad, Colonel Aureliano Buendía was to remember that distant afternoon when his father took him to discover ice. – Gabriel García Márquez, *One Hundred Years of Solitude* (1967; trans. Gregory Rabassa)

---

1 Go back and reread the first sentence and the quote that began the Introduction to this book ("the hook for the book"). If done correctly, they should have been a successful inducement for you to read the rest of the book.

e. Lolita, light of my life, fire of my loins. – Vladimir Nabokov, *Lolita* (1955)

f. Happy families are all alike; every unhappy family is unhappy in its own way. – Leo Tolstoy, *Anna Karenina* (1877; trans. Constance Garnett)

g. It was a bright cold day in April, and the clocks were striking thirteen. – George Orwell, *1984* (1949)

A "hook" is particularly important in a cover letter. It serves the same purpose as a "hook" in a novel or nonfiction book. You want to pull the reader into your letter and give her or him a reason to read the entire letter – beginning to end. Below are six different kinds of "hooks" you may wish to consider for your cover letters:

Type of Hook	Examples
Quotation	• John Steinbeck once said, "I have come to believe that a great teacher is a great artist...." • When Cesar Chavez said "We need to help students and parents cherish and preserve the ethnic and cultural diversity that nourishes and strengthens this community – and this nation," he highlighted one of the most significant issues in American education.
Anecdote	• It was a wheelchair-bound junior high school teacher who changed my life forever...in less than five minutes. • There is nothing more frightening than a 275 pound football player about to knock you out.

Question	• What is the single-most critical question all teachers must answer… every school day?
	• Are you looking for an intensely curious teacher who is never satisfied with "same old, same old?"
Interesting fact	• This year nearly 150,000 new graduates will be looking for teaching jobs across the United States.
	• In ancient Egypt, The Books of Instruction contained rules for the well-ordered life and elements of morality that included justice, wisdom, obedience, humanity and restraint.
Simile or metaphor	• When I walked into student teaching I was like a small bird just learning how to fly.
	• Teaching is not the filling of a pail, but the lighting of a fire.
Mystery	• The classroom was a cacophony of noise. Then the principal walked in, saw what was happening, and smiled.
	• Two words made all the difference…all the difference in the world.

FROM THE PRINCIPAL'S DESK:

"Your cover letter must have some sort of 'hook' - something that will grab my attention immediately and make me want to read the rest of the letter."

Let's take a look at how a "hook" can improve a typical cover letter. In the following example, notice how the addition of a "hook" (the *After* letter) significantly improves a standard opening paragraph often seen in many cover letters:

Cover Letter: *Before*

Lay Dee Gaga
123 Virtuoso Lane
Harmony, CA 93435

April 21, 20__

Ms. Melody Tune, Principal
Treble Clef Elementary School
492 Singsong Way
Tuba City, AZ 86045

Dear Ms. Tune:

I am applying for the third grade teaching position posted on your web site last week. I am currently in my student teaching semester at Honeybee Elementary School and will graduate from Hardwork University in May with a bachelor's degree in Elementary Education. My current GPA is 3.68.

Cover Letter: *After*

Lay Dee Gaga
123 Virtuoso Lane
Harmony, CA 93435

April 21, 20___

Ms. Melody Tune, Principal
Treble Clef Elementary School
492 Singsong Way
Tuba City, AZ 86045

Re: Third Grade Teacher

Dear Ms. Tune:

She was barely four feet tall, but she was a giant in my life.

Mrs. McDonald, my sixth grade teacher, could only reach halfway up the white board, yet she reached me in ways I've admired to this day. She never accepted second best – if a paper wasn't right she send it back for a "Do over" and if an assignment wasn't complete, it wasn't accepted. She prodded, she pushed, and she provoked – and in so doing I discovered that learning wasn't a passive process, but rather an active one, one that demands individual responsibility and high personal standards. It's something I've embraced throughout my entire teacher training program. It is my fervent wish to bring that attitude and that philosophy to the third grade students at Treble Clef Elementary School.

I think you can see a significant difference between the two letters. The first letter is "same old, same old." It's a familiar opening that has been used a thousand times (no, a million times) before and one guaranteed to put any administrator into a deep slumber, The second, letter, on the other hand, grabs the reader's attention from the start and embellishes the initial sentence with a personal story that just begs to be read. The reader has been effectively "hooked" and is now being reeled in by a very competent writer/fisherman/teacher.

Second Paragraph

This paragraph may be the most critical one in the entire letter – it is, in so many ways, the heart and soul of a good cover letter...a letter that truly sells the candidate, rather than one that simply summarizes and reiterates the contents of the resume. The "message" of this paragraph must demonstrate how your skills, talents, and experiences can be used to address the specific needs of the school or district. Most applicants, in their haste to craft a letter that can be used with almost every application packet, will generalize excessively – using a lot of words, but not saying very much.

> ## FROM THE PRINCIPAL'S DESK:
>
> "Know the district you are applying to. Districts like to know the candidate is 'in to' them, not just sending out applications to all districts just to apply. We like to feel wanted by the candidate as well as the candidate feeling wanted by us."

Your job here is to show the reader how you are able to perform the tasks which the specific job requires. The fact that you want a job and that you need the income that goes along with that job are secondary to the administrator's wants and needs. If this paragraph is all about you then it will fail...miserably. Once again, you are *selling* the reader on how you will benefit her or his school; you are not *telling* her or him all about you.

As anyone in advertising will tell you (and, as you will remember from Chapter 3), it is critical that you highlight the *features* and *benefits* of a product (In this case, *you* are the product). In order to do that, it is often necessary to put yourself in the shoes of a potential buyer and look at a product from their point of view. For example, look at these samples of ads where the emphasis is on a product's *features* and *benefits*:

- "Saving people money since 1936" (Geico Car Insurance)

- "Naturally light and fresh taste." (Lipton Tea)

- "This is not just a bed. It's the sleep experience that will change your life." (Sleep Number Beds)

- "We select the softest leather, to make you feel at home." (Singapore Airlines)

- "Ignite your taste buds." (Lay's Potato Chips)

Now, let's take those same advertising lines and rewrite them as though they were telling us something, instead of selling us something. You'll quickly notice the difference.

- "Our car insurance costs less than the car insurance from other companies."

- "Our tea really tastes good."

- "We make the best beds in the country."

- "The seats in our planes are covered in leather."

- "Our potato chips are good."

> ## ✓EXTRA CREDIT:
>
> For practice in writing <u>selling</u> statements (instead of <u>telling</u> statements) you might enjoy the following homework "assignment." Write down five facts about yourself. For example, "I have taught multiplication facts to an entire third grade class," or "I student taught in a tenth grade social studies class." For each of those facts, write a *selling* statement – a statement that focuses on the *features* and *benefits* of you. For example, "Third graders were able to master their multiplication facts with speed and accuracy," or "An interdisciplinary social studies program was implemented resulting in an overall improvement in mid-term grades of 19%."

In order to <u>sell</u> yourself there are several questions you must answer in this all-important second paragraph (Don't try to answer ALL of these, but you must address several of them):

- What are the *benefits* of me?
- What specific *features* can I bring to this school?
- What do I know about this specific institution and how can I address their needs?
- What skills, talents, or experiences do I have that are germane to this school, and just this school?
- What is innovative or distinctive about what I can offer?
- What value will I bring to this specific school or district?
- Why should this school or district "buy" me?

The most important question you can answer in this paragraph is one always in the mind of every single administrator who will read your cover letter. If you don't provide the answer to this question, you will never get any farther in the application process. That question is:

"What can you do for me?"

Far too many applicants are focused on answering another question – a question that has no place in a cover letter, a resume, or anywhere in the entire application packet. Focus on answering this question (as so many other applicants will) and you, too, may discover that the road to that all-important first job may be very long and very tiresome. Trust me when I tell you no administrator is interested in your answer to this question:

"What do you want?"

It is essential you keep your focus on the value and benefits you would bring to a specific school or district. Obviously your value and benefits will be different from school to school simply because every school is unique; every school is different. Please don't assume that every elementary school is identical; neither should you assume that every secondary school is the same. Each has their own unique and singular characteristics. The successful applicant for a job will effectively address those singular features with a letter written specifically for, and to, that school.

Third Paragraph

In sales, this would be called the "call to action" or simply the "Close." This is where you politely request that some form of action be taken on the part of the reader. For example, you may request an interview, you may ask for some form of follow-up to your application packet, or you may ask for a specific appointment. This is not where you want to be brazen or brash, but rather where you want to display some degree of confidence. In other words, this is where you want to ask, "Given your review of my qualifications, would you like to interview me?"

Good closing paragraphs are frequently shorter than the other two paragraphs and they invite a call to action on the part of the reader. All too often, teacher candidates approach this paragraph with some degree of fear and trepidation. As a result, they tend to finish off their cover letter with one or more passive statements. This is not, however, where you want to end on a passive note; rather, you want the reader to know you are confident that your unique set of skills and talents can best serve her or his specific needs. Here are some examples:

> **Common Close:** "I look forward to hearing from you at your earliest convenience."

> **Better Close:** "I look forward to interviewing with you to discuss how I might address your unique challenges."

> **Common Close:** "I hope you will review all my application materials, which are included with this letter."

> **Better Close:** "To meet your specific needs, I've included several additional materials."

Here are some examples of excellent closing paragraphs:

...

After you have had a chance to review my application packet, I believe you will agree that I am well prepared to teach chemistry at Longview High School. Thank you for your time in reviewing my credentials. I welcome the opportunity to interview with you soon.

Sincerely,

Bonnie Ann Clyde

…

Enclosed, as requested, is my complete application packet. I would enjoy meeting with you and members of the selection committee to share my excitement and enthusiasm for this new teaching venture. It is the kind of professional challenge I relish. Thank you, in advance, for your consideration.

Sincerely,

Marty Graw

…

My student teaching evaluations from Dr. Williamson and Mrs. Brookshire have been consistently "Excellent" and "Exemplary." I am sure they would tell you how deeply committed I am to establishing an invitational and cooperative classroom. I am equally enthusiastic about sharing that philosophy in the Butterworth School District. In that regard, I look forward to meeting you.

Sincerely,

Polly Ester

Good cover letters are like good magazine advertisements – they are designed to highlight the attractive *features* and *benefits* of a product (e.g. a car, a form of insurance, a bed, a cup of coffee…and YOU). Successful ones aren't a simple listing of factual data; instead, they appeal to the senses, they address the inner needs of a potential buyer, and they describe how a buyer's life will be better as a result of purchasing (or hiring) a particular product (or future teacher).

Bottom line: sell, sell, sell!

✓EXTRA CREDIT:

Get a stack of popular mass-market magazines such as *Vogue, Vanity Fair, Better Homes and Gardens, InStyle, Glamour, People, Sports Illustrated,* and *Ladies Home Journal.* Go through all the advertisements and tear out 20-30 of the ads you particularly enjoy. Take a look at the wording in each of those ads. If the ad is particularly effective, you'll undoubtedly notice that it has a focus on a product's *features* and *benefits* moreso than it does on that product's facts and details. Effective ads emphasize the benefits of a product to the reader rather than the specifics (e.g. ingredients, parts, colors, design, shape). Your cover letters should do the same.."

INSIDER TIP

Drop your cover letter into a word cloud generator (e.g. http://www.wordclouds.com/; http://www.wordle.net/; https://tagul.com/) and see what key words are emphasized. If the most important words aren't what you want to be known by, then some revising may be in order. By the same token, if certain words are over-emphasized, think about how they could be reduced in your cover letter. Another good idea: drop your resume into a word cloud generator, too.

A TOUCH OF HUMOR

Sometimes candidates overstate the obvious (perhaps to fill up space). Here's a good example:

"Experience: Any interruption in employment is due to being unemployed."

Chapter 20

High Caliber Blunders That Will Shoot You Down

If you have ever been in a committed relationship with someone, I'd like to invite you to take a few minutes and think back to the first time you met that person. What were you aware of? What caught your attention? What stood out about that individual? If you are like most people, there were any number of first impressions that you noticed and that you liked about that person. Maybe it was a smile. Maybe it was a unique sense of humor. Maybe it was a certain look, a sparkle in the eyes, or the tilt of a head. Whatever it was, there was something there that captured your attention; something that made you say, "Hmmm, this could be interesting!" or "I think I'd really like to go out with this person." And, so you did.

Interestingly, psychologists tell us that we often form an initial impression about a person in two seconds (yes, two seconds) after meeting her or him. We rapidly decide if someone has features or qualities that are in alignment with what we expect from friends or potential mates. Most of those initial impressions are made as a result of prior experiences with many different individuals in our lives. The more contacts we have with people the better able we are to make decisions about other people (potential spouses, for example).

And so it is with cover letters. The reader of a cover letter is, quite often, someone who has read many cover letters in their professional careers and thus has acquired a wealth of background knowledge about what good cover letters should have and what bad cover letters often exhibit. Just like you made a quick decision about that person sitting next to you in your English Composition course, a school administrator will make a quick decision about you based on the quality of your cover letter. If your cover letter is full of deficits, you'll never get a second chance... you'll never get a second date (the interview)!

FROM THE PRINCIPAL'S DESK:

"I have had many candidates use the same cover letter to apply for multiple positions. When you read a cover letter where the candidate starts by saying they hope to get a teaching position in a school, that is not your school, it is once again easy to eliminate them from any consideration."

In my conversations with principals I gathered data on the most common mistakes applicants make in their cover letters. Several of these will sound familiar because they are also blunders that crop up on resumes, too. Several are unique to cover letters, simply because administrators have seen them time and time again on hundreds of thousands of those documents. Please consider the observations of these administrators as serious "food for thought" in the construction of your own cover letters. Know that your competitors will be making these mistakes (effectively taking themselves out of the running for any open position) and that you can stand above the competition by systematically excluding any and all of these errors from your cover letter. Simply put, you will gain someone's attention by the simple act of ensuring that not a single one of the following blunders ever creeps into one of your cover letters. True, the content of your cover letter is critical, but no more so than the way in which that content is delivered. Make the delivery without error and you will be providing the recipient with excellent customer service. In turn, the recipient (the building principal) may want to place an order for your participation in a formal interview.

1. <u>**You Knew This Was Coming – SPELLING!**</u>

Rule #1: Use the Spell Check feature on your word processing program… but don't over-rely on it. A spell checker doesn't know the difference between "their", "they're", and "there"…but you should. Rule #2: Invite at least four other people to read your cover letter to see if everything is spelled correctly. Make sure at least two of those individuals are not college students or close friends. Working adults in your family or neighborhood are strongly suggested.

A TOUCH OF HUMOR

Oh yes, this was in one applicant's cover letter:
"I speak English and Spinach."

2. ...And This One, Too – GRAMMAR!

Re-read Rule #1 above (substitute the phrase "grammatically correct" for the phrase "spelled correctly").

3. Uh, Oh – Wrong Name/Wrong Title

Check (and double check) the name typed on your cover letter. Make sure it is the correct individual to whom the letter should be sent. Also make sure that the person's name is spelled correctly (you might want to triple-check this). Also, make sure that the person's title is correct (Is the person a principal or the assistant principal; the superintendent or the assistant superintendent; the Human Resources Manager or Supervisor of Personnel?). Drill down into the school or district web site to be sure you have the correct person and that person's correct title. There's no excuse for sending your cover letter to the wrong person. In a pinch, call the district office and ask someone who your letter should be sent to. Also ask them how to spell the person's name.

FROM THE PRINCIPAL'S DESK:

"Names that are misspelled on the cover letter automatically go in the NO pile as well as cover letters with typos and poor sentence construction."

4. Too Many !!!!!!!'s

O.K. you've done lots of great things during student teaching! You've accomplished some incredible tasks during your field experiences!! You've volunteered for all sorts of community functions involving children!!! But, enough with all the exclamation points. Besides being overkill, it's visually distracting, very self-serving, and it's giving me a splitting headache. Stop it.

5. Summarizing Information in the Resume

Don't duplicate information from your resume in your cover letter. Remember that your cover letter should be designed to enhance and compliment your resume – it doesn't replace the resume. The resume will provide a reader with an overall perception of who you are as a potential teacher; the cover letter (if read) will simply confirm that impression.

6. Stating What YOU Want

Here's a hard truth – you are NOT applying for a teaching position in order to get a job; rather you are applying in order to fill an opening the school or district has available. This entire process is not about you, it's about satisfying a need that a school or district has. If you frame your cover letter in terms of what you want, then you are setting yourself up for failure. On the other hand, if you can craft a letter that is more focused on how your specific qualifications are in line with the requisites of the posted position, then your chances for success mushroom exponentially. You must satisfy a school or district's needs, not your own personal needs.

> **NO:** "I want this position because I think I'm the best qualified teacher."

> **YES:** "I would like to contribute my qualifications and enthusiasm in helping fourth grade students at Highpoint Elementary School achieve higher levels of reading comprehension and appreciation."

A TOUCH OF HUMOR

Oh, if only I had had the intestinal fortitude to write what this candidate did:

"My family is willing to relocate. However not to New England (too cold) and not to Southern California (earthquakes). Indianapolis or Chicago would be fine. My youngest prefers Orlando's proximity to Disney World."

7. "Cookie-cutter" letter

In an effort to save time many applicants make a serious and fatal mistake. They try to craft an all-purpose cover letter; that is, a cover letter that can be printed out and sent along with every application they write. Whether they submit applications to ten schools or a hundred, the cover letter is always the same. It's generic, superficial, and bland.

Indeed, one of the worst mistakes you can make is to craft a "one size fits all" cover letter. That letter sends a very powerful signal – "I am way too lazy to take the time to write an individual and unique letter to each and every school or district I'm applying to." You try to cut corners by coming up with a cover letter that can be used for every school in the Western Hemisphere – a letter that tries to be all things to all people. The problem is that these letters stand out like a proverbial sore thumb – any administrator who has read more than a few cover letters will be able to spot these phonies in the blink of an eye. Now is the time to do what so many of your competitors will not – make each cover letter personal, unique, and distinctive.

FROM THE PRINCIPAL'S DESK:

"[Cover letters] are often addressed to the wrong contact person, or the wrong district, or are obviously a form letter used for all districts. Take the time to mention something unique about our district in your letter."

Look at the difference in the beginnings of the two letters below. Which one do you think would get the more positive response?

A.

Dear Sir or Madam:

I would like to obtain a teaching position in your district. I am just completing my student teaching assignment and would look forward to bringing my skills to one of your schools.

B.

Dear Mr. Templeton:

The Eagle River High School web page has posted "Success in Learning; Success in Life" as the school's mantra. If you are looking for an English Composition teacher who will promote that motto in both word and deed, then I believe I have something unique to offer you.

The first letter is junk mail (it could have been sent to any school in the country); the second letter is specific (It is targeted to one very specific school). The first letter will, most likely, find its way into a wastebasket. The second letter will, most likely, find its way into a "YES" pile. Bottom line: Be specific, never generic.

8. **Not Doing Your Homework**

Now, here's a tip that will surely put you "heads and shoulders" above your competition – something that will make you stand out in a most positive way. Research the school or district web site and be sure to reference an item from that site in your cover letter. This is a sure way to let a reader know that you have done your homework and know something specific or unique about that school.

For example, let's say you wanted to send me an email, but you knew nothing about me. On the other hand, you want to make a special request (No, I will not loan you any money for this semester's tuition!) so, instead of addressing the email to "Dear Sir" you decide to discover something about me via my web site (www.anthonydfredericks.com).. One of the things you might note is that I've written a lot of children's books. So, to get into my good graces (and ensure my attention), you begin a message with the following: "Dear Dr. Fredericks: As the author of many award-winning children's books (including *Under One Rock* and *Desert Night, Desert Day*), would you be able to recommend one or two writing instruction books for a novice author?"[1] The fact that you've taken the time to learn something about me makes me much more inclined to read

---

1   Compare this opening with the following generic opening: "Dear Sir: I have an idea for a children's book. Can you recommend some writing instruction books for me?"

your message in its entirety…and to possibly respond in kind. That extra research can make all the difference in whether your message is actually read or systematically discarded. If your message sounds like it is being "spammed" to many other individuals or institutions, then it is highly likely that it will be ignored by many other individuals or institutions.

9. **Eliminating the "Hook"**

- DULL! DULL! DULL!: "I am finishing my student teaching requirements and would like to teach math in a middle school next year."

- EXCITING! EXCITING! EXCITING!: "When Nelson Mandela said, 'Education is the most powerful weapon you can use to change the world,' he highlighted a persuasive truth about the influence of good teachers."

Don't make the mistake of starting your cover letters the way almost everyone else will. Don't begin with the obvious, the commonplace, or the mundane. Grab the reader's attention with a vibrant, rich, and unique opening – one that commands attention and entices her or him to read the next sentence, and the next sentence, and the next.…

10. **An Avalanche of Clichés**

The dictionary defines "cliché" as "a trite phrase or expression; something that has become overly commonplace." In short, a cliché is something everyone uses on their cover letter…everyone sounds the same. On the other hand, you want to stand out – you don't want to be one of the crowd, but rather one of a kind. If you use the same phrases and terms all your competitors do you will become considerably less than memorable. And that's not what you want.

Strike the following from your vocabulary and from all your cover letters. Please.

- "I was responsible for…." (Guess what, we're all responsible for something when we go to work. State specifically what you did to make kids academically successful.)

- "I'm a team player." (Unless you're a member of an NBA basketball team, this doesn't mean anything.)

- "I'm self-motivated." (If you're planning to be a classroom teacher, this will be quite evident. There's no need to state the obvious.)

- "I have great communication skills." (When someone cuts me off in traffic, I have some pretty good communication skills, too! What specific communication skills (in education) do you possess: (for example) the ability to explain complicated formulas, the ability to counsel kids in crisis, or the ability to talk with angry parents?)

- "I have a strong work ethic." (Even after more than four and a half decades of teaching experience, I'm still not sure what this means.)

- "I'm a problem-solver." (Everyone who has ever changed a flat tire on a busy highway is a problem-solver. What specific educational problem or problems did you tackle and solve.)

- "I have a proven track record." (So did American Pharoah, but he was a race horse.)

- "I assisted in X task." (OMG – Saying you "assisted" is the kiss of death! State specifically how you took initiative and got things done.)

FROM THE PRINCIPAL'S DESK:

"Whenever I see 'I assisted...' or 'I assisted my cooperating teacher in...' I immediately toss the resume in the NO pile. I don't want people who 'assisted;' I want teachers who take charge and show real instructional initiative."

11. "Tell, No Sell"

Once again, remember that one of the primary objectives of a cover letter (as with a resume) is to sell the experiences you will be able to bring to a school or district. Don't make the all too common mistake of simply listing all your experiences – that is, "telling" a reader about what you did or what you learned. That's what your competition will do.

Instead, take the time to focus on selling what you will bring to a school as a response to their immediate needs. As an example, let's take a look at some magazine advertisements that do a very good job of selling a product, instead of merely telling you about the product:

- "Our world revolves around you." (Air France)
- "Why enjoy just one cookie when there's a whole stack in front of you?" (Geico Insurance)
- "Switch to AT&T and get an iPhone for free." (iPhone)
- "The lush things in life. I live for it." (Maybelline)
- "Savor the dark." (Ghiradelli Chocolate)
- "Some things are full of hormones. We're not." (Oscar Mayer Natural Turkey)

12. **<u>Too Long</u>**

Repeat after me: "One page. Three paragraphs. The end." Thank you.

FROM THE PRINCIPAL'S DESK:

"Limit your cover letter to one page. Administrators don't have time to read multiple pages."

13. **<u>Forgetting to Replace a School Name or Specific Position</u>**

Take the time to write a unique and personal letter to each school or district and this will issue not be a problem for you. Trying to save time by writing a generic cover letter will, most definitely, truly mess up your chances of getting an interview – much less a job.

FROM THE PRINCIPAL'S DESK:

"One of the biggest mistakes teacher candidates make on their cover letters is when they neglect to post the correct name of the district/school they are applying to. Often the candidate is applying to multiple districts and he/she neglects to change the school's name."

14. <u>Writing in the Negative</u>

Phrases such as "I didn't....", "I won't....", and "I can't...." often frame you as a person who lacks skills, talents and desires. They cast you in a negative light and hint at a personality that would be unwelcome in most schools. Always put your language in positive tones – celebrate what you have accomplished, positively promote your commitment to teaching, and herald how your attitude and disposition are always forward-thinking and celebratory. The key is to make your cover letter sound upbeat and engaging – a positive tone almost always ensures a positive response (such as an invitation to an interview).

15. <u>Boasting; Over Confidence</u>

Only one person had the right to say, "I am the greatest!" – Muhammad Ali. Please remember that you are, most likely, about to complete your student teaching semester. You are technically a pre-service teacher – a novice, a beginner, a neophyte, a rookie. While you may have had a plethora of experiences working with kids, you're not yet a full-fledged teacher. Please don't make the mistake of thinking otherwise. An overabundance of confidence or a boastful attitude will surely turn off any principal reading your letter. Be confident, not arrogant. There's a big difference between the two terms and that difference will reveal itself in the tone you establish in your cover letter.

A TOUCH OF HUMOR

One candidate noted the following in his cover letter:
"I have technical skills that will take your breath away."

16. <u>Listing References</u>

On-line applications will often ask you to list several references. That's O.K. However, it's not necessary (or even required) that you list the availability of references on your cover letter. That doesn't mean that you shouldn't have references; just that you don't need to include them on your letter. If you are called in to an interview, you may be asked to bring along several letters of recommendation. Therefore, it's always appropriate to request those letters during the application process. Every principal will assume that those letters will be made available if requested as an element of the interview process. There is absolutely no need to include the names of your references on the cover letter (or any references to those references).

#

Think of cover letters as the icing on the cake (your resume is the cake, by the way). A well-constructed cover letter adds some additional flavor, a little bit of spice, a few decorations, and an extra enhancement to your most important document – the resume. The right ingredients can ensure that the cake (the resume) stands out from all the other cakes. Yes, it is possible to have a good cake without frosting, but with the addition of a few (delicious) ingredients you can create a masterpiece that will be savored and remembered for a long time. Yum!

FROM THE PRINCIPAL'S DESK:

"I like a cover letter that exudes passion in relation to the teaching profession. Being able to list a variety of life experiences to support this passion is a bonus."

Chapter 21

<u>Your Cover Letter Checklist</u>

For each cover letter you plan to send out make a photocopy of the following checklist (e.g. 11 different cover letters = 11 checklists). Before sending (via e-mail or postal mail) each cover letter, complete the following checklist to be sure you have met all the essential rules for cover letter writing. Please edit your letter as necessary before sending it.

General

❏ I have checked (and double-checked, and triple-checked) the spelling in this document.

❏ I have had someone else check (and double-check) the spelling in this document.

❏ I have checked (and double-checked) the grammar in this document.

❏ I have had someone else check (and double-check) the grammar in this document.

❏ The name listed at the top of the letter is identical to that on the top of my resume.

❏ I have used the same font in this letter as I did on my resume.

❏ This letter answers "the most important question" on the mind of the reader.

❏ I have made sure I've written to real person, not a position.

❏ I have limited this letter to single page (no more).

❏ I have limited the letter to three paragraphs (no more, no less).

❏ I have used a plethora of action verbs to describe my experiences and knowledge.

❏ I have focused on the reader's *needs*, not on my *wants*.

❏ I have created a letter that is unique and specifically directed to single school/district.

❏ I have placed an emphasis on *selling* my achievements, not merely *telling* about those achievements.

❏ I have addressed specific qualifications as listed in the job announcement.

❏ I DID NOT summarize my resume in this letter.

❏ I have not used any educational clichés in this letter.

❏ I have clearly demonstrated my enthusiasm for the position.

❏ I have eliminated any statements beginning with "I believe," "I feel," and "I think."

❏ I have included information that clearly shows my familiarity with the school/district.

❏ I have emphasized how or what I can contribute to the school/district.

The Following Elements are Included

❏ Header

❏ Date

❏ Inside address

❏ Subject line

❏ Professional salutation

Body - 1st Paragraph

❏ I have included an appropriate "hook."

❏ The paragraph uses action verbs

❏ The paragraph is active, rather than passive.

Body - 2nd Paragraph

❏ This paragraph emphasizes my features and benefits for the school

❏ I have put a premium on *selling*, instead of *telling*.

Body - 3rd Paragraph

❏ I have emphasized a call to action.

❏ I have asked for an interview.

In Conclusion

❏ I have included an appropriate complimentary closing ("Sincerely," "Respectfully").

❏ I have identified myself with my formal name.

❏ The name listed at the bottom of the letter is identical to that on the top of the letter.

❏ The name listed at the bottom of my letter is identical to that on my resume.

❏ I have signed my name exactly as printed.

❏ I have signed my name in blue or black ink.

❏ As appropriate, I have included an "Enclosure" notation.

A TOUCH OF HUMOR

Here is the kind of candidate I want working in my school:
Why should we hire you?
"I bring doughnuts on Friday."

Chapter 22

<u>Sample Cover Letters</u>

Following are several sample cover letters for your review. Just like with the sample resumes in this book, use these as examples that incorporate all the advice in the previous chapters. Please don't use them as all-purpose templates to be copied, duplicated, and sent out to hundreds of schools. For each one you will notice a slight change in formatting with each letter; just as you will notice different experiences and different qualifications highlighted in each document. Feel free to use any of these designs, but be sure to make the information in YOUR letter unique, personal, and specific to a single opening in a very specific school or district.

Tyler D. Edelson
874 Windemere Drive • Lexington, SC 29072 • tylerd@xxx.net
(803) 888-9999 (H) • (803) 123-4567 (C)

April 17, 20__

Dr. Michael F. Gerund
Morganton Area School District
820 North 4th St.
Morganton, NC 28655

Re: Third Grade Teacher

Dear Dr. Gerund:

Henry Brooks Adams once wrote, "A teacher affects eternity, he can never tell where his influence stops." With a diversity of in-school experiences, competence in working with disadvantaged youth, and a willingness to go "above and beyond" the usual array of teacher responsibilities, I, too, would like to influence the students of the Morganton Area School District. I believe you will find my qualifications appropriate for the position.

The Morganton Area School District web site states, "Success for every student" as their educational goal. Having had numerous opportunities to work with disadvantaged youth in several urban environments I believe I can competently address the educational needs of your third graders through a coordinated program of differentiated instruction in concert with positive behavior management. I don't promise instant solutions; rather I can assure you an instructional plan focused on class discussions, open-ended questions, and cooperative learning - a program designed to help the youngsters of Morganton achieve high levels of academic success.

A review of the accompanying resume will demonstrate my commitment to struggling learners as well as a background of experiences dedicated to high scholastic achievement. I look forward to the opportunity of meeting with to share my enthusiasm, zeal and dedication to excellence in teaching. Thank you in advance for your consideration.

Sincerely,

Tyler D. Edelson

This applicant starts off his cover letter with a dynamic quote (a great "hook") - something everyone would agree with. He then goes on to demonstrate how he would emphasize the context of that quote in his own classroom. He backs up that quote with one taken directly from the district web site - demonstrating that this letter is tailored for a specific district.

(Ms.) Chris P. Bacon
999 Liberty Way, Apt. 33A • Portland, OR 97215 • chrisbacon@xxx.net
(971) 555-5555 (H) • (971) 444-4444 (C)

May 9, 20__

Mrs. Janice Perkins, Principal
Shady Hook High School
9378 Timberline Drive
Portland, OR 97223

Re: Secondary Social Studies Teacher

Dear Mrs. Perkins:

Are you looking for a social studies teacher willing to "go the extra mile" for each and every student; one never satisfied with the status quo; and one who is keen on building lifelong learners? If you are, then I would like to respectfully submit my formal application for the recently posted position with Shady Hook High School.

My professors at Portland State University have labeled me as "a go-getter," and "an eager beaver." Truth be told, I am passionate about my responsibilities as a teacher - believing that good learning begins with an exceptional role model. My desire to be the best teacher possible coupled with my appetite for educational excellence has engaged me in a plethora of challenging and demanding experiences throughout my teacher training program. I believe your recently re-designed social studies program offers a unique opportunity for me to share my enthusiasm and hands-on learning philosophy with your students in unique and achievement-oriented ways. I earnestly seek to become part of an instructional team dedicated to the role of social studies in everyday life.

As a sincere and committed teacher I can assure you of a true dedication to Shady Hook's instructional goals. I look forward to the opportunity of sharing that devotion and desire with you in the very near future. Thank you in advance.

Respectfully,

Chris P. Bacon

> The applicant asks a very powerful question as her initial "hook." She then goes on to answer that question in a very persuasive way. She also takes the time to bring in some "outside opinions" - the voices of her college professors to demonstrate that she is a legitimate and highly qualified applicant.

Roel ("R.J.") Ramos

86395 Bison Road   (307) 555-9999 (H)
Cheyenne, WY 82007   (307) 555-6666 (C)

<u>rjramos@xxx.net</u>

April 2, 20__

Mr. Leroy Smithton, Principal
Prairie View Elementary School
820 Cottonwood Drive
Lusk, WY 82225

Re: Fifth Grade Teacher

Dear Mr. Smithton:

"The whole art of teaching is only the art of awakening the natural curiosity of young minds for the purpose of satisfying it afterwards." - Anatole France

In the letter posted on Prairie View's web site, you told parents that one of the chief responsibilities of teachers was to stimulate and encourage the natural curiosity of children. As you will note in the enclosed resume, I am passionate about inquiry-based learning, higher level thinking, and purposeful question-asking. I have had several unique teaching opportunities where I have satisfied my own curiosity about learning in concert with advancing "hands-on, minds-on" endeavors that facilitate and satisfy self-initiated scholastic endeavors. My philosophy is to create a highly interactive and inquisitive classroom atmosphere that promotes self-discovery and self-direction.

Beyond student teaching and the required 150 hours of field experience at Yellowstone State University, my goal has been to acquire a wide range of educational experiences with a diversity of students. To that end, I have had several exceptional opportunities to work with many different styles of learners - offering individualized and extracurricular support, technological assistance, and 'Best Practices" teaching strategies to insure the academic success of youngsters. As epitomized in the quote above, I continue to strive to "awaken" and "satisfy" natural curiosity - both for myself as well as for my students.

I look forward to the opportunity of working closely with your team of teachers in addressing your educational goals. Thank you for your time and attention. I anticipate hearing from you soon.

Sincerely,

R.J. Ramos

It is clear that this applicant has taken the time to write a letter that is unique and clearly directed at one school...and one school only. This is not a "mass-produced" letter, but rather one that is backed by some thorough research on the immediate needs of a particular school and how one prospective teacher can meet those needs.

Shanda Lear
9627 Watt Place, Light City, MD 21205   shandal@xxx.net • (443) 555-7777

May 28, 20__

Dr. William Norris, Principal
Perfection Middle School
98648 Shoreline Drive
Bethany Beach, DE 19930

Dear Dr. Norris:

I'd like to be your next math teacher.

As a recent graduate from Outstanding University with an extensive and varied background in mathematics education in concert with numerous experiences in working with disadvantaged youth, I believe I can offer Perfection Middle School quite a lot in their quest for "a quality learning environment that promotes character, fosters responsibility and challenges students to achieve their potential."

Here are some specific qualifications I can bring to your school:

- **I embrace a student-centric curriculum.** Students achieve best when they are actively engaged in the dynamics of their own learning. I work tirelessly to ensure that reality.
- **Teacher as facilitator.** Good teachers help students set and reach their own educational goals - he/she does not do that for them. I embrace a "partnership" approach to teaching and learning - giving students responsibilities that help them succeed.
- **Higher-level thinking.** I believe that questions are more important than answers. I am known for asking a plethora of high-level questions that facilitate thinking and cognition.
- **Trust and respect.** I have always believed that students should be treated as human beings, not as residents of a classroom to be criticized (or endured).

Enclosed is my complete application packet. I would enjoy meeting with you to share my enthusiasm for this new position. It is the type of professional challenge I relish and embrace. Thank you for your consideration.

Sincerely,

Shanda Lear

Look at the powerful opening this applicant uses (no beating around the bush here). She also demonstrates respect for the reader's time by including a list of bulleted points that go above and beyond the data that might appear in her resume (but, more general than specific). The letter may be short, but there is a lot of power here!

Erica R. Dawson

575-555-9999   89-B Saguaro Way, Tucumcari, NM 88401   dawsone@xxx.net

March 23, 20__

Mrs. Karen Cooper, Principal
Vista Bonita Elementary School
8979 Gila Road
Rio Rancho, NM 87144

Re: Kindergarten Teacher

Dear Mrs. Cooper:

When the governor of our state said, "Success is the American Dream. And that success is not something to be ashamed of, or to demonize," I knew I had chosen the right profession.

My goal has always been to provide a learning environment that ensures, not only the academic success of youngsters, but also their personal and emotional success as well. I am a strong advocate of "Whole Child Learning" and have invested my undergraduate years at Roadrunner College in a wide variety of educational ventures to prepare me for the challenges of the 21st century classroom. I would truly welcome the opportunity to bring my skills and commitment to the Kindergarten students at Vista Bonita. These would include an invitational learning environment, authentic assessment, thinking over content, mutual respect, varied instruction, and adaptive learning. So too, would I welcome the chance to share my passion and enthusiasm for teaching with Vista Bonita parents. I can assure you of an innovative academic program that engages every student.

My professors and supervisors have recognized me as a "dedicated and devoted teacher always willing to go the extra mile." Over the past four years I have established myself as a take-charge educator who always gets the job done no matter what the challenge or circumstances. I am confident I can contribute mightily to the academic milieu of Vista Bonita. I shall welcome your call to discuss this opportunity in more detail.

Respectfully,

Erica R. Dawson

> Several elements come into play here: A direct quote from a recognized leader, a direct match between the qualifications of the applicant and the immediate needs of the school, a strong philosophical emphasis, recommendations from other educators, and a powerful call to action. This is a letter that will truly rise to the top of any applicant pool.

Appendix A

Your Other "Resume"

Two stories:[1]

1.

Stewart Griffin was in the middle of his student teaching semester at Hidden Harbor College. He was an outstanding student and both his college supervisor and cooperating teacher sang his praises. It was clearly evident that he was going to be a most outstanding secondary social studies teacher. In fact, word had gotten around the county that more than one principal was interested in hiring him – even before he completed his student teaching requirements. He was that good!

One of the traditions at Hidden Harbor College was the annual "Spring Bash" at a local pub in the downtown area. Each year there was a different theme, and this year the theme was "Pirates." Students were encouraged to come dressed as pirates, talk like pirates, eat like pirates (no silverware), and behave like pirates. Stewart and his friends spent several days putting together some elaborate pirate outfits – complete with bandanas, eye patches, ragged pants, and fake parrots (on their shoulders). The festivities started at 8:00 and Stewart and his crew arrived shortly after 9:00. It didn't take them long to get into the action and they were singing, dancing and tossing back more than a few mugs of beer in the process.

One of Stewart's friends took a photograph of him leaning against the bar with his distinctive eye patch, an equally distinctive pirate hat, a plastic sword in one hand and a large stein of beer in the other. The photo found its way onto Facebook the next day and it and several other photos from the all-night celebration were quickly circulated around campus.

---

1   These two stories are true. The names have been changed and minor details have been modified in order to protect the identity of the individuals involved.

The existence of Stewart's pirate photo soon came to the attention of the Chairperson of the Education Department who requested an immediate meeting with Stewart. She told Stewart that he was in violation of both College policy as well as the Department's policy regarding "personal maturity," "use of prudent judgement," and "ethical, moral character." She then told Stewart that his student teaching placement was terminated and that he was being dismissed from the teacher education program – effective immediately.

Stewart got a lawyer and sued both the College and the Education Department for unfair dismissal. He lost the case. As a result he was not able to complete his teaching degree, nor will he ever be allowed to obtain teacher certification in that state.

Oh, one more thing – Stewart was 24 years old (legal drinking age)!

2.

Mr. Hansen, the principal at Rolling River Elementary School, received approval from the District Superintendent to advertise for a new second grade teacher as a result of increased enrollment in the district. He posted the position on a Monday and by Friday afternoon he received 389 applications – many from out of state.

He began reviewing all the applications that Saturday. His initial review of resumes eliminated 297 individuals from further consideration. He lamented the fact that so many of those resumes were filled with spelling errors (His last name suffered through six different incorrect spellings), grammatical mistakes, and formatting miscues.

He then read through the remaining 92 applications focusing on the accompanying cover letters. This process resulted in the elimination of 56 applications from further review. He then spent the remainder of the weekend carefully and patiently reading every element of the final 36 applications. By the time Monday morning rolled around he had narrowed the field to four finalists – four candidates he wanted to call in for interviews. He could only hire one.

Interview appointments were scheduled for the final four people – after which two were deemed insufficiently qualified for the position. The final two applicants were Jason Thomas and Amanda Ridley – both of whom had stellar student teaching experiences, solid letters of recommendation, and a plethora of activities and experiences that went far beyond the usual requirements of pre-service teachers. He called both of them back in for another round of interviews. Once again, they both excelled!

He asked both of them to come back (a third time) and teach a sample reading lesson for a group of Rolling River teachers. The teachers gave both Jason and Amanda superior marks and pleaded with Mr. Hansen to hire both of them – they were that good! But, he could only hire one.

It was the day before the June school board meeting – the meeting at which Mr. Hansen had to make a recommendation of one of the two finalists for the 2nd grade position. He read the applications again and again, but still couldn't decide. Throughout the day, he anguished over his quandary – it seemed almost impossible to decide between two very qualified and very capable teachers.

Finally, that night, he remembered something Amanda had shared during one of her two interviews. In response to a question about the use of technology in the classroom she had casually mentioned that she maintained three or four email addresses. Something about that comment stuck in his mind and he decided, on a whim, to check them out.

He discovered that Amanda did, indeed, have multiple email addresses. One of those addresses was IWANTDARKLUV@ XXXX.net. The next evening Mr. Hansen presented his recommendation to the school board and Jason Thomas was immediately approved for the second grade position.

Your Digital Footprint

Throughout this book I've offered you advice, suggestions and strategies for you to create a dynamic resume and an equally impressive cover letter. You might think that these two documents, if prepared according to the ideas in this book, will ensure that you will get a job interview. You might think that this book, in concert with its companion volume *(Ace Your Teacher Interview: 149 Fantastic Answers to Tough Interview Questions* [Indianapolis, IN: Blue River Press, 2016]), will turn you into that one candidate every principal wants to hire. You might think that these resources along with your impressive record in college will virtually guarantee you a job in the school of your dreams. You might think that you will have it made.

Wrong!

That's because, for all the work you put into your resume and cover letter, you have also been spending considerable time (over the past four years) crafting a "resume" that might have more to say about who you really are than any documents you prepare and send off in response to a job posting. As you are no doubt aware, you have been building a digital footprint – a record of all your online actions, activities, communications, things you send or post about yourself and others, websites you visit, texts, pictures, and posted videos. In short, your "resume" or digital footprint, is all the information online about you either posted by you or by others, whether intentionally or unintentionally. And that digital footprint, because it is often created in a casual, relaxed atmosphere can often reveal more about you than a carefully crafted paper resume designed to impress people (i.e. people you would like to work for). Now the question is: "What kind of digital footprint are you leaving behind for others to follow?

A TOUCH OF HUMOR

I'm not sure this is a candidate I would want to call in for an interview:

"Experience: Demonstrated ability in multi-tasting."

A friend of mine (I'll give her the name "Dr. Claire"), who teaches education courses at another college, once had a student (I'll give him the name "Bob") who absolutely hated her course. He thought there were far too many papers to write, there were too many required classroom visits in the local schools, Dr. Claire's lectures were too intense, and her standards were far too stringent. It was known as a challenging course, but Bob was convinced that all those assignments and all those tests were far too much – especially for a methods course. He also didn't like Dr. Claire very much.

At the end of the semester when grades were posted (Bob received a "2" [C] in the course.), he wrote several "juicy" comments about Dr. Claire on a popular web site. One of those comments was: "You have to kiss her a__ to get a good grade in her course." All his friends thought Bob's comments were funny and they were circulated around campus.

Just before graduation, Bob began sending out his resumes and cover letters in order to secure an interview in the local area. He desperately wanted to teach and was looking forward to lots of interviews and, hopefully, lots of job offers. He was despondent when, time after time, he kept getting "Thanks, but no thanks" letters from principals or, in many cases, no response at all. What Bob didn't know was that his "innocent" comment had surfaced and had been shared with several administrators in the local area. The general feeling was that the negativity expressed in that comment was a "red flag" – an attribute no administrator wanted in her or his school, no matter how impressive the candidate's resume or cover letter. The sad story is that Bob didn't get a single interview for a job.

All because of one online comment.

You may not realize it, but what you say or do online can be seen by others. Students have been kicked off sports teams and even out of college for posting pictures of themselves doing or saying inappropriate things online. Others have been arrested and required to register as sex offenders for sharing inappropriate images via the internet or through text messages. And, as you've read, prospective teachers have sacrificed their entire professional careers as a result of inappropriate, insensitive, and unacceptable postings.

✓EXTRA CREDIT:

Google yourself. See what comes up.

I hope you're also aware that once you post something online, it's difficult, if not impossible to get it back. You might have a friend who can take some of that material down, but there are ways for others to retrieve that data. And, the things you said or posted may have been copied, saved, or sent to others. In short, once it's online, it's online in perpetuity! And, if you are in the running for a coveted teaching job, I can assure you that your digital footprint will be accessed and will be checked. It, not your formal resume, may ultimately determine whether or not you are hired.

Think about it: Your digital footprint – your other resume!

INSIDER TIP

Your Digital Footprint

- You are what you post
- You give up your privacy
- Everything is permanent
- Everyone is watching
- Anyone can learn about you online
- Everyone will (or can) know
- It frequently carries more "weight" than any formal resume

Appendix B

<u>Online Applications</u>

Many school districts, along with many counties and states, are using online applications as a way to simplify the hiring process. The obvious advantage for candidates is that posting your teacher resume online places it where thousands of potential employers and recruiters can see it. If your credentials are first rate, you can increase your chances of having your documents read by many potential employers.

INSIDER TIP

Whenever possible, save your resume and cover letter as a PDF document. If it is acceptable to send your materials as PDF files (Word documents, as attachments, are often the preferred method), then do so. The advantage is that the unique formatting (of your resume, for example) on a PDF file won't get messed up when your document is opened on different computers.

For example, New York has The Online Application System for Educators – a cloud-based application serving school districts throughout New York State. Districts can view applicant specific information including resumes, cover letters, transcripts, portfolios, and more. Candidates are able to apply to specific positions using one application and/or have an option of granting all participating school districts access to their application.

The benefits of this system include the following:

- No cost to applicants create a profile and apply for jobs.
- Available job openings throughout the state can be viewed.
- Saved applications can be updated at any time.

- Applications remain active for one year.
- Accessibility from any computer with internet access.
- Applicants can easily edit and update their application.
- An applicant's information is secured with SSL technology.
- Job are updated (and made available) daily.
- A directory of participating school districts is made available.

A TOUCH OF HUMOR

This might be an interesting person to interview (or not) for a teaching position:

"Work Experience: Responsibilities included checking customers out."

Suffice it to say, online applications are a "win-win" for both applicants and school districts. If, for example, you are considering applying to schools in a state distant from where you live or will be submitting a teaching application for an international position, then an online process may be the only way to get your resume and cover letter in front of the people doing the actual hiring. Although the crafting of resumes and cover letters remains the same, here is some specific information relative to online documents.

1. Follow all the directions very carefully. Be sure you enter the appropriate information in the appropriate fields.

2. Complete all the fields – even those that are not required.

3. You may be asked to take an optional assessment test online. Don't pass this up.

4. If you are asked to e-mail your resume be sure to include your name and the exact teaching job you are applying for in the subject line of the e-mail. This helps recruiters identify that the e-mail is from a prospective applicant.

5. Knowing your resume will be read on a computer it would be important for you to make all of your hyperlinks live. This would

include your email address, a professional site (such as LinkedIn), or a personal web site (such as wix.com). This makes it easier for a reader to access additional information.

6. As enumerated earlier in this book, make sure your format is simple and clean. Fancy bullets, italics, bolding, and graphics often do not convert very well.

7. Remember that this is not a text message. Don't use any abbreviations such as FYI (for your information), "u" (you), or emoticons (;-). Spell everything out.

8. It is strongly suggested that you send your resume as a Microsoft Word document. Some schools or districts may not be able to view documents in PDF or JPEG formats. A Word attachment (of your resume and cover letter) is often preferred over other transmissions. Be sure to check beforehand so that you can submit the appropriate documents in the appropriate manner.

If you are sending your documents as attachments to an e-mail, it would be appropriate to provide a brief introduction in the body of the e-mail. This introduction should contain your contact information in the event the recruiter needs to let you know that your resume did not upload properly. For example:

Dear Dr. Drinker:

I am interested in the 10th grade English teacher position as posted on the Orange County Department of Education web site. With outstanding evaluations from my college supervisor and cooperating teacher in concert with a rich variety of volunteer positions in community youth programs, I believe I can offer your students an exceptional learning experience. Attached are my resume and cover letter for your consideration. Please confirm receipt by contacting me at 949-555-1234 or wxyz@gmail.com. Thank you in advance.

Respectfully,

Ginger Ayl

INSIDER TIP

When you assign a file name to your resume do it as follows: "[First Name] [Last Name] Resume" - it makes it easier for readers to locate and file this important document.

Appendix C

<u>Web Resources</u>

I am often asked about web sites candidates can consult for additional tips and strategies in preparing resumes and cover letters. While *Ace Your Teacher Resume (and Cover Letter)* is designed as an "all-in-one" package of techniques, strategies, and designs for these critical documents, you may find it advantageous to check out some of the following web sites for additional information.

As you know, the internet is constantly evolving. The following web sites were functioning and active at the time of the writing of this book. I have purposely selected sites that have been around for a while, are extremely popular, and that have established themselves as viable sources of resume and cover letter information. Please be aware, however, that URLs may change, web sites may move or be discontinued, and other factors may influence these listings. However, that said, you will discover a wealth of additional readings and information on these sites that will be useful in crafting your documents.

The following listings are not ranked – they are only listed in alphabetical order.

A+ Resumes for Teachers (http://resumes-for-teachers.com/teacher-resume-examples.htm) – You'll discover a wealth of sample resumes and cover letters on this site. The folks who run this site also offer a unique resume writing service that will produce an individually tailored resume just for you.

About Careers (http://jobsearch.about.com/od/sampleresumes/a/teacher-resume-examples.htm) – Here are teacher and other education-related resume examples to use to get ideas for your own resume, including early childhood education, teaching abroad, and related positions such as youth worker and recreation coordinator.

Classroom Caboodle (https://classroomcaboodle.com/teacher-resource/elementary-school-teacher-resume/) – There's lots of information (plus a couple of videos) on this site to help you write your resume. Although some of the suggestions conflict with information in this book (the use of color and graphics, for example), many of the tips are very good.

Job-Interview-site.com (http://www.job-interview-site.com/Job-Interviewing-tips/teacher-resume-examples) – Get free samples of 15 different teacher resumes including art teacher, kindergarten teacher, math teacher, music teacher, preschool teacher, special education teacher, substitute teacher, elementary teacher, English teacher, librarian, and others.

Live Career (https://www.livecareer.com/resume-samples/teacher-resumes) – Here, you'll find tips and specific advice on how to craft a resume that will increase your chances of getting an interview. You'll also find teacher resume samples that you can use to get an idea of formatting options that may suit your style.

Monster (www.monster.com/career-advice/article/sample-resume-elementary-teacher) – Elementary teachers can access a resume template (similar to the format used in this book) for their own document. There's also a link for a sample resume for middle school teachers.

Pinterest (https://www.pinterest.com/explore/teacher-resumes/) – Yes, it's all here! Hundreds of ideas plus lots of sample resumes fill this site. Check it out - there's a lot of great stuff here.

Resume Bucket (https://www.resumebucket.com/sample-resumes/teachers/) – Not only does this site show you how to write a good teacher resume, it also provides more than 60 different sample of resumes for all categories of teachers.

Resume Genius (https://resumegenius.com/resume-samples/teacher-resume-example) – In this writing guide, four teacher resume samples are provided - middle school, elementary school, preschool, or substitute teacher. The site also outlines the different methods candidates can use to create an achievement-oriented resume.

Resume-Resource (http://www.resume-resource.com/teacher-resume-examples/) – Lots of tips, loads of ideas, and a whole bunch of good advice are waiting for you're here. Also, there are links to lots of free samples.

A TOUCH OF HUMOR

This is one of my favorites:

"Application: How large was the department you worked in with your last company? A: 3 stories."

Index

Read on for a peek at
another important job-hunting
book by bestselling and award-winning
*author **Anthony D. Fredericks**.*

Ace Your Teacher Interview:
149 Fantastic Answers to
Tough Interview Questions

"This should be required reading
for all Education majors."

(Amazon.com 5-star review)

Available from Blue River Press

(www.cardinalpub.com)

or wherever fine books are sold

Chapter 1

<u>What You Need to Know About Interviews</u>

For most of my life I was a long-distance runner. In high school, college, four years in the armed services, graduate school, and through most of my teaching career I continued to run long distances. For me, one of the best parts of the day was when I came home from a long day of teaching. I'd throw on a pair of shorts and a t-shirt, lace up my running shoes, and take off along the rural roads where we lived for a run of six or eight miles. Occasionally I'd run up and down rolling hills, along dusty lanes, or around the perimeter of a public golf course. Every so often I'd lope over to the local high school to do some interval work on the track. About once a month or so (more in the summertime) I would enter and run a 10K race. Occasionally I would get a trophy or a medal or some sort of special certificate for my placement in the race. However, it wasn't the awards that were important to me, but rather the opportunity to run faster than I had in a previous race at the same distance.

I had learned early in my running career that the more effort I put into my daily runs the better I would do in the races I entered throughout the year. Running 70-80 miles per week – track workouts, endless hill climbs, and long runs through undulating countryside – were necessary if I was to lower my times or do well in any forthcoming long distance races. As a former college coach put it succinctly, "There are only three ways to be a good long distance runner – run, run, run!"

And guess what – there are only three ways to be successful in a teacher interview – prepare, prepare, prepare! If all you do is put together a resume and send out letters to a dozen schools and keep your fingers crossed you may be very disappointed…and very jobless! You need to prepare…you need to go the extra mile (or two). Here's the key to getting the teaching job you want:

You need to distinguish yourself in some positive way from other candidates vying for the same position(s).

Getting a teaching position must be an active process – it should never be a passive project. Doing what everyone else does (sending out endless batches of applications, correspondence, letters of recommendation, and resumes) will seldom guarantee you a job. You need to set yourself apart from the crowd, you need to distinguish yourself as a candidate of promise, and you need to demonstrate initiative, drive, and enthusiasm. Anything less and you'll be seen as *one of many* rather than *one of a kind*!

The Themes of a Teacher Interview

When a principal, superintendent, or committee interviews potential teachers there are several themes they have in mind. While this book provides you with 149 of the most frequently asked questions in an interview (along with suggested responses), it's important to remember that all of these questions and all of the other parts of a teacher interview are centered on eight basic themes. By knowing these universal themes – and by preparing for each one – you can assure yourself of a positive reaction by a prospective employer.

One way to look at each of these eight themes is to imagine each as part of a sales message – each one is designed to highlight and showcase your skills, abilities, and attitudes in the most favorable light. Each one is designed to separate the mediocre from the good and the good from the great. Everything you do, everything you say, and everything that occurs in a teacher interview is tied to these themes – separately and collectively.

I encourage you to read through these themes. Then, try some of the following:

- Think of each one, and develop a personalized approach to each one.

- Write or record a response – how would your talents, skills, philosophy, and abilities address each theme?

- Take apart your resume and reassign your personal information to every theme.

- Tell a friend (not in education) how you would present yourself in regards to the themes.

- Write each theme on an index card and carry them around with you. Pull the cards out during the course of the day and review them…and review your responses.

In short, prepare yourself to respond – in both word and actions – to these key themes and you'll be ready for any interview…and any interview question.

Eight Interview Themes

Every principal or hiring authority wants to know several things about any teacher candidate. Your success in that interview will be based in large measure on how you fulfill each (and all) of the following themes. Those who get hired are those who fulfill these basic educational themes.

1. A Passion for Teaching

When I interviewed elementary and secondary principals for this book and asked them to identify the single-most important characteristic in a quality teacher candidate, guess what they all told me? You guessed it – "A Passion for Teaching!"

Do you have a passion for teaching? How do you demonstrate that passion? What activities, projects, or assignments have you engaged in that demonstrate your passion for teaching? What have you done that shows you are willing to go the extra mile for students? What have you done that demonstrates your sincere commitment to teaching? Where have you gone above and beyond? Did you do something in student teaching beyond the ordinary? Did you do something during your pre-service years that went above and beyond your college's requirements for teacher certification? What truly excites you about teaching? What "floats your boat"?

2. Skills and Experience

One of the first things you need to do in any interview is to establish your ability to do the job. In a nutshell – *Can you teach and can you teach effectively?* In most interviews these will be the initial set of questions you'll be asked. Many of these questions will be factual in nature and will provide you with an opportunity to highlight your skills and talents and how they will be used in a classroom setting. This is when you must offer specific information rather than generalities. It is also the time to be completely objective about yourself – with confidence and assurance.

INSIDER TIP

Tony Beshara, who manages a professional recruitment and placement firm in Dallas, Texas says that the answer to "Can you do the job?" accounts for the first 20% of the hiring decision. In short, a candidate must convince an interviewer that she/he is capable of doing the job very early in the interview process.

How do you put together a lesson plan? What do you do when a lesson isn't working? Describe one of your best lessons? What will you bring to the teaching profession? Why should we hire you? Why do you want to be a teacher? What did you learn in student teaching? Please don't make the mistake of assuming that these are easy questions – they are not! They are often asked near the beginning of the interview because they help "set up" the rest of the interview. Positive answers to these questions help ensure the success of the entire interview.

INSIDER TIP

Every interviewer wants to know about the potential and specific benefits you will bring to the school or district. Thus, it is important to give examples of your strengths that relate to the school's needs. For example, instead of saying "I like to teach science," say something like, "I've been known to get even the most reluctant of students interested in science through a 'hands-on, minds-on' inquiry-based approach to science education."

3. Likeability

Here's a basic truth you may find difficult to believe. The most important factor every interviewer is looking for in a candidate is NOT the breadth and depth of her or his skills, education, or talents. It's likeability! In a recent review of more than 100,000 face-to-face interviews there was not one candidate hired who wasn't, at first, liked by the people doing the interviewing and hiring. You might think that one's personality would be of less value than their teaching prowess, but such is not the case. Simply put, people get hired because they are liked.

INSIDER TIP

According to Tony Beshara (see above), "The number of extremely qualified, excellent candidates that weren't hired because they weren't initially liked by the interviewing or hiring authority defies logic and common sense."

What are your three greatest strengths? What are some of your hobbies or free time activities? How do you handle criticism? How did you handle disagreements with your college supervisor? What makes you the best teacher for this position? Who is the greatest influence on your life? What is the biggest mistake you've ever made? Interestingly, hiring decisions are based more on personality factors than they are on skill factors. You may be the best qualified candidate, but if you aren't the best liked, then the position will probably go to someone else.

4. Student Orientation

Several years ago I was part of a team of people interviewing several candidates for a teaching position. I distinctly remember one young man who spent the entire 45-minute interview talking about his accomplishments, his resume, his background, and his prowess in writing exciting lesson plans. After he left, I remarked to my colleagues that not once, in those 45 minutes, did he ever refer to students. Not once did he ever use the word "students." It was apparent that he was more interested in presenting himself than he was in teaching students. Candidates without a strong student orientation are candidates that don't make it any further in the hiring process. Without that orientation, without that commitment to student life, and without that desire to work hand-in-hand with youngsters nobody ever gets hired as a classroom teacher.

How do you motivate an unmotivated student? How do you assess students? Tell us about your toughest student – how did you handle him/ her? How do you address cultural diversity in your classroom? What do you enjoy most about working with kids? What are some challenges you've had in working with kids? Besides student teaching, what other work have you done with youngsters? Come to an interview with a strong and sincere student orientation and you may well walk away with a job offer.

5. Professionalism

You're about to get a college education. Great! But, that doesn't mean your learning has ended. The field of education is changing rapidly – new technology, new standards, new curricula – lots of new stuff. Your willingness and eagerness to continue your education is a key factor in your "hireability." Candidates who assume that just because they have a degree their education is over are those who never succeed in an interview. Any principal or administrator wants to know that you are a constant learner – that you are willing to keep learning through graduate courses, in-service programs, on-line seminars and webinars, membership in professional organizations, books, magazines and journals, and a host of other professional opportunities that signal your eagerness to keep your education moving forward.

Where do you see yourself five years from now? What are your plans for graduate school? In what area of teaching do you still need some improvement? Tell me about a book you've read recently. What are the essential traits of a good teacher? Do you belong to any professional organizations? One of my lifelong mantras as a teacher has always been: "The best teachers are those who have as much to learn as they do to teach." Be prepared to demonstrate how you might embrace this quotation in your everyday activities.

6. Management and Discipline

You've probably seen classrooms in which students were orderly, work was productive, and a sense of purpose and direction filled the room. You might also have seen classrooms that were chaotic, disruptive, and seemingly out of control. Maybe you were even a student in one or both of those classrooms at some time in your educational career. Principals are vitally interested in how you plan to manage your classroom. Your management skills and discipline policy will be vitally important in the decision to hire you. Know that you will be asked more than one question in this area. Read, research, and review everything you can – your success here will frequently be a major deciding point.

✓ EXTRA CREDIT:

According to research from several observers, teachers in a typical classroom lose about 50 percent of their teaching time because of students' disruptive behavior. Be prepared to discuss how you would address this issue somewhere in the interview.

To establish a positive classroom environment, share what you will do the first few weeks of school with your students. How do you create and maintain positive rapport with your students? How would you deal with a student who was always late to class? Describe your discipline policy in detail. Describe some classroom rules you would use. To many administrators nothing is more important than a well-crafted discipline policy and a well-articulated management plan. Be prepared to share your thoughts on both.

FROM THE PRINCIPAL'S DESK:

"School districts place a tremendous emphasis on discipline and classroom management.... They want to feel confident that you, as a new teacher, have a good, sound, fair method of class management. You can't wimp out in this area."

7. Lesson Planning

A lesson plan is only a guide. A well-designed lesson plan is flexible, subject to change, and reflective of the individual needs of each and every student in the classroom. A good lesson plan provides an outline for the accomplishment of specific tasks, while at the same time allowing for a measure of flexibility in terms of student interests and needs. You need to demonstrate to any interviewer your familiarity with lesson design as well how you are able to tailor lessons to the specific instructional needs of your students. Be prepared to be detailed and specific as well as flexible and accommodating.

Please relate the process you go through when planning a typical lesson. Please share some ways in which you have assessed students. What are the essential components of an effective lesson? Think of a recent lesson you taught and share the steps that you incorporated to deliver the lesson. Share your process of short and long-term planning for delivering effective instruction. Think of a lesson that was ineffective or did not meet your expectations – what adaptations did you make to address the lesson? How do you infuse technology to enhance your instruction? It's critical that you provide an interviewer with insight into your lesson planning, lesson delivery, and lesson assessment. Anecdotes and examples must be critical elements of your responses.

8. Flexibility

Can you 'roll with the punches?" Can you "go with the flow?" Can you "change directions in midstream?" Can you "bend in the wind"? All these questions have to do with perhaps the most significant attribute of any good teacher – flexibility. Interviewers want to know that they will get the most "bang for the buck" – that you can handle a wide variety of classroom situations, a wide range of teaching challenges, and a wide array of changes, modifications, or alterations – all at a moment's notice. Your willingness and eagerness to present yourself as someone who can adapt without getting flustered or change without getting upset is a key attribute – an attribute that can often "nail" the interview.

Are you willing to teach at another grade (elementary)? Are you willing to teach another subject area (secondary)? How would you handle a fire drill in the middle of your favorite lesson? What if we brought in a brand new reading series next week, what would you do? Are you comfortable with change? Would you be willing to work in an after-school program? Administrators are always interested in individuals they can use in a variety of situations. The willingness to be flexible and the desire to quickly adjust to change are both positive characteristics valued in any school.

* * *

The themes above show up in every teacher interview. Practice them, be prepared for them, and review them on a regular basis. Your preparedness – like that of a long-distance runner - will help you run the extra mile, beat the competition, and set a personal record - getting the teaching position you want!